W9-BKT-896

Shelton State Libraries
Shelton State Community College
DISCARDED

THE TOWN THAT FOOD SAVED

HD
9008
.H37
H49
2009

THE TOWN
THAT FOOD SAVED

HOW ONE COMMUNITY FOUND VITALITY
IN LOCAL FOOD

BEN HEWITT

DISCARDED

RODALE

Notice

Mention of specific companies, organizations, or authorities in this book
does not imply endorsement by the author or publisher, nor does mention
of specific companies, organizations, or authorities imply that they
endorse this book, its author, or the publisher.

Internet addresses and telephone numbers given in this book
were accurate at the time it went to press.

© 2009 by Ben Hewitt

All rights reserved. No part of this publication may be reproduced or
transmitted in any form or by any means, electronic or mechanical, including
photocopying, recording, or any other information storage and retrieval system,
without the written permission of the publisher.

Rodale books may be purchased for business or promotional use or for special sales.
For information, please write to: Special Markets Department,
Rodale Inc., 733 Third Avenue, New York, NY 10017

Printed in the United States of America

Rodale Inc. makes every effort to use acid-free ⊗, recycled paper ◉.

Book design by Christina Gaugler

Library of Congress Cataloging-in-Publication Data

Hewitt, Ben, 1971-
    The town that food saved : how one community found vitality in local food /
Ben Hewitt.
        p.   cm.
    ISBN-13 978-1-60529-686-9 hbk
    ISBN-10 1-60529-686-4 hbk
    1. Food supply—Social aspects—Vermont—Hardwick. 2. Food industry and
trade—Vermont—Hardwick. 3. Sustainable agriculture—Vermont—
Hardwick. 4. Entrepreneurship—Vermont—Hardwick. 5. Hardwick (Vt.)—
Economic conditions—21st century. I. Title.
HD9008.H37H49 2009
338.1'974334—dc22   2009034294

Distributed to the trade by Macmillan

2   4   6   8   10   9   7   5   3   1   hardcover

We inspire and enable people to improve their lives and the world around them

For more of our products visit **rodalestore.com** or call 800-848-4735

For Penny, Fin, and Rye.
And anyone who likes to eat.

CHAPTER ONE

If you come into the town of Hardwick, Vermont, from the east, you come in on Route 15, weaving through a series of curves that begin as gentle sweeps and become progressively sharper until you find yourself leaning in your seat, the view through your windshield tilted just a few degrees off its axis. That's the Lamoille River on your right, gurgling and churning over water-worn stone and gravel; it cuts a course through the center of town, and there's a nice little walking bridge that crosses the water. It's on Main Street. It's not hard to find.

On your left, the land rises steeply from the highway's shoulder. It's mostly wooded, but just outside town, you can see where the hillside washed away a few years back; it's since been reinforced with a massive pile of rocks, but the homes visible at its crest still look disturbingly vulnerable, as if the slightest shift will send them bouncing down the hill to splinter across the roadway.

Hardwick sits in a shallow hollow; the town and its 3,200 residents live in the shadow cast by Buffalo Mountain, which rises to nearly 3,000 feet at the southwest corner of town. Buffalo Mountain is at once craggy and lush, populated by a mix of eastern hardwoods: birch, beech, ash, and the state's vaunted sugar maple. There is no road to the top, although all-terrain vehicle trails crisscross its flanks.

If you claw your way to the top of Buffalo Mountain and look out over the town, you'll see how Route 15 becomes Main Street, and Main Street lasts for about a quarter-mile before it hits the town's only traffic light, which consists of a single flashing orb at the junctions of Routes 14 and 15. If you turn right, continuing on

15, you'll immediately pass the former home of the Amateur Boxing Club, a garage, a gun shop, a pizza house, and a lumberyard, in that order. A bit farther out, there's a bank and a tractor-repair business. A Ford dealership. A gas station. If you go straight through the light onto 14 South, you'll pass two auto-parts stores, a school, a cemetery, and a series of modest residences. In either direction, you'll see how you could drive through Hardwick in two minutes or less, pushing on the accelerator as the speed limit rises again to 50 and the road unfurls across the lush Vermont countryside, drawing you in and on, helping you forget about the small town you just left behind.

Here's what you won't see: Over the past three years, this little hard-luck burg with a median income 25 percent below the state average and an unemployment rate nearly 40 percent higher has embarked on a quest to create the most comprehensive, functional, and downright vibrant local food system in North America. In the process, Hardwick, Vermont, just might prove what advocates of a decentralized food system have been saying for years: that a healthy agriculture system can be the basis of communal strength, economic vitality, food security, and general resilience in uncertain times.

Indeed, the sudden growth in Hardwick's ag infrastructure has been nothing short of explosive, with numerous food-based businesses and organizations settling in the region, seeking to become a part of the town's answer to the vexing question of what a healthy food system should look like. Vermont Soy Company. High Mowing Organic Seeds. Jasper Hill Cheese. True Yogurt. Claire's Restaurant and Bar. Pete's Greens. Vermont Food Venture Center. The Center for an Agricultural Economy. The Highfields Center for Composting. Honey Garden Apiaries. While a few of these enterprises have been quietly operating and growing for the past 5 to 10 years, most of them have arrived in the past 3 years, bringing nearly 100 jobs to a region that very much needed 100 jobs.

No, you won't see this from the summit of Buffalo Mountain, but you can see it along Hardwick's block-long Main Street business district, where local food-based enterprises (Claire's Restaurant and Bar, the Buffalo Mountain Food Co-op, the Village Diner, the Center for an Agricultural Economy) dominate, in some cases inhabiting buildings that had long sat idle. This is not the end of it. Soon, the Vermont Food Venture Center, a shared-use commercial kitchen and product development, processing, packaging, and shipping facility, will open in Hardwick, providing a place for small-scale producers to create and distribute value-added goods made with local ingredients, saving them the massive expense and hassle of installing such a facility on their own properties. And the nonprofit Center for an Agricultural Economy recently purchased 15 acres of prime agricultural land only two blocks from downtown; plans call for establishing what the center has dubbed an Eco-Industrial Park, which will potentially include shared office space for the town's ag-based businesses, a year-round, indoor farmers' market, farm and garden demonstration sites, a communal composting operation, and rental plots for budding farmers.

The recent growth in Hardwick's ag-based commerce is notable for something else: These outfits are, by and large, operated by youthful entrepreneurs possessing a surprising degree of business acumen. These are not the back-to-the-land dropouts of the region's 1970s' homestead agricultural revolution, smoking joints, hand-milking goats, and bartering Grateful Dead bootlegs for bunches of warty carrots (well, okay, perhaps some of this is happening); these are, by and large, graduates of our nation's elite liberal arts colleges who have sought ways to apply their six-figure educations to occupations rooted in the soil. They spend their days tending livestock, fields of lettuce, and racks of cloth-bound cheddar and their evenings convening to quaff beers and brainstorm the next step forward for this little settlement that just might be the most important food town in the United States.

If that seems like an outsize claim for a small town with a hard-bitten reputation, one need only consider the most recent outbreak of bad food news. The rise in energy and fertilizer prices has led to double- or in some cases triple-digit food inflation. In early 2008, the price of rice nearly doubled . . . in a single month. Milk prices are up nearly 100 percent in two years; ditto for wheat and corn prices. And with the average piece of American food traveling nearly 1,500 miles from farm to table, it's likely to only get worse as finite fossil-fuel reserves continue to shrink. On average, every calorie that lands on your plate soaked up 11 calories of fossil-fuel energy as it was sown, grown, harvested, processed, and shipped. When the price of those 11 fossil-fuel calories doubles, then triples, and finally rises exponentially, the cost of that single calorie of nourishment will rise, too.

It's no great secret that over the past century, America's food system has become increasingly industrialized and centralized. It's an economy of scale that has served us well, at least in strictly economic terms. In 1930, the average American family spent 24.2 percent of its income on food. That number has declined in every single decade since; by 2007, it had fallen to 9.8 percent. Of course, there are hidden costs in the form of health problems wrought by processed foods and an agriculture industry that has become heavily reliant on subsidies paid out of your taxes. But the fact remains: Until very recently, our food has never been cheaper. It has also never been more corrosive to our health and environment.

There are other problems with our centralized food system. Most critically, it's vulnerable to energy-supply disruptions, terrorist attacks, widespread outbreaks of food-borne illness, and any unforeseen emergency that disrupts the constant flow of trains and trailers. And recent events suggest that it simply might not be able to keep up with a population that's growing at the rate of three million mouths annually. Consider this: In 2001, the United States had a $14.3 billion agricultural surplus. By 2005, that surplus had shrunk to $3.8 billion.

It might seem crazily, disturbingly pessimistic to think that the United States, a nation renowned for abundance, could run short of food. But in 2007, driven by drought, biofuels, and the simple limits of soil, global grain stocks declined to a level not seen in 34 years. Given that 2008 saw continued drought in major grain-producing nations such as Australia and biblical flooding in the midwestern United States, it's unlikely the situation will resolve itself soon. In fact, much of the steep run-up in rice prices last spring was due to many rice-exporting nations exporting less. The result wasn't merely an expensive pot of rice; many Costco superstores limited sales of the grain to their customers. That's right: Food rationing, in the United States, in 2008.

What conclusion might we draw from this? Unfortunately, it isn't pretty, because the fact is that our nation's food supply has never been more vulnerable. And we, as consumers of food, share that vulnerability, having slowly, inexorably relinquished control over the very thing that's most critical to our survival. We have become utterly dependent on a supply chain that is entirely beyond our control, in no small part because it typically starts a half-continent away. There is no single action, corporation, or agency that can secure this fragile infrastructure and deliver us a steady supply of nourishment. We could debate endlessly and vigorously over the root cause of this tragic disconnect, and perhaps there's some value in that. But the truth is, we've arrived at this crisis from many and varied directions. Is it the modern archetype of agriculture as a corporate entity, with its deep pockets and unquenchable appetite for profit? Yes. Is it the intricate web of governmental regulations and subsidies that have supported the food-as-a-commodity model? Yes.

Is it the inexorable chipping away of our land and skills base, to the point where the vast majority of us no longer possess the means or the knowledge to produce even a head of lettuce? Yes. Is it our willingness to allow these things to slip through our fingers in favor of the ease of supermarket shopping? Yes.

The cheap-food boom has been seductively comfortable for us all. Let's face it: Farming is damn hard work, typically done for damnable pay. By relinquishing this burden, by handing the reins to the corporations, we relieved ourselves of a lot of backaches, sunburns, and financial strains. We struck a deal: The agribusinesses got a guaranteed chunk of our income and our full faith in their ability to keep us sustained. In return, we got to pursue lifestyles that don't revolve around soil and toil and that allow us a measure of leisure time unprecedented in human history. In early 2009, American television viewing reached an all-time record of a stunning 151 hours per month. That's more than five hours per day, and let's be clear about something: You and I don't get to sprawl across the sofa masticating pork rinds and watching *American Idol* unless someone else is growing the food.

As long as the corporations keep their end of the bargain, it's a pretty sweet deal, presuming one overlooks the pallid, depleted nature of the foodstuffs they're providing. But it's becoming increasingly obvious that they won't be able to hold up their end of the bargain forever or, if recent events are any indication, even for much longer. This leaves us facing a rather daunting truth: The fact is that we need to rethink our entire food-supply chain for reasons of economic security, health security, and even social security. We need to reinvent how we grow and distribute food; we need to re-scale and decentralize.

It is hard to grasp the enormity of this task on a national scale. It is no less challenging or important than wrenching our economy and way of life from the clutches of petroleum. And yet there has been no consensus on the issue; indeed, there has been little in the way of serious debate among anyone beyond the growing but still very much in the minority community of locavores who bounce around farmers' markets with their reusable organic-cotton satchels. To be sure, they are an important part of our agricultural renewal. But between them and a healthy national food system lie thousands and thousands of acres of corn and soy and wheat sown in depleted soils and coaxed to life with chemical fertilizers, waiting to be harvested, amalgamated into shelf-stable concoctions, packaged, and trucked to a nation of people who have already forgotten it wasn't always like this. And who can't imagine that it won't always remain so.

To understand how Hardwick has gotten to this place and to know where it might go from here, it is necessary to understand where it has been. In many ways, it is not unlike scores of other rural communities scattered throughout the American landscape, built on industries that long ago packed up their bags and left. In Hardwick, that industry was granite, and it's hard to overstate how much vibrancy, excitement, and money the stone provided the town. Over a period of three decades, spanning the late 1800s to the early 1920s, nearly 300 granite companies operated in the Hardwick area, mining the rock veins that run like spiderwebs throughout the surrounding hills. By 1918, the largest of these outfits, the Woodbury Granite Company, was the biggest granite operation in the world. It supplied the stone for the state capitols of Pennsylvania and Wisconsin, as well as Chicago's City Hall and Cook County Courthouse. Even a cursory exploration of the region's densely wooded hills will reveal the century-old detritus of the trade: lengths of frayed and rusted cable, pieces of corroded metal shorn from some mysterious tool or another, impossibly heavy

slabs of discarded stone jumbled together like a god's game of
pickup sticks.

These were raucous times, marked by the swagger and pent-up
energy of men who spent the week engaged in hazardous duty and
needed to blow off a little steam on weekends before returning to
the constant dangers of tumbling stone and the pervasive granite
dust that caused silicosis-induced lung disease, known throughout
the region as "stonecutter's tuberculosis." The accident reports of
the day read like gruesome parodies of themselves, bearing phrases
such as "crushed between stone blocks," "wound around machinery gearing," "crushed between two railroad cars," "struck by flying metal from an exploding steam boiler," and "premature quarry
explosion." If you'd just maneuvered through your week without
having had your name attached to one of these scenarios, you'd
want to kick up your heels a little, too.

And, if you were a granite worker in Hardwick, Vermont, during these halcyon days, you'd have had the money to do it. A gran-
ite-cutter's union founded in the late 1800s ensured that wages
were generous by the standard of the day, and by 1920, at the
height of the boom, union members pulled down $8 per day, more
than double the typical laboring wage of the era. How'd they
spend their loot? Why, in the timeworn manner of working men
the world over. On Saturday nights, pockets thick with cash, the
granite crews descended upon downtown from the numerous
boardinghouses on Hardwick's fringes to give the bars and restaurants a rousing business. To satisfy the enormous thirst and appetite of its laboring population at the peak of granite fever, the town
boasted 18 drinking and eating establishments, and the boisterous
"work hard, play hard" ethic that pervaded the town earned it the
moniker Little Chicago. It is rumored that for a brief period,
Hardwick, Vermont, boasted more bars per capita than any town
in America.

The high times did not last. In the early 1920s, the granite bubble deflated with alarming speed, the victim of shifting architectural tastes toward reinforced concrete and facing stones that significantly reduced building costs and eliminated the challenge of shipping 80,000-pound blocks of stone. The demise of Hardwick's granite industry dealt the region a tremendous blow, and it marked the beginning of an extended economic downturn from which the town has yet to fully recover. Its reputation as a hardscrabble town was further cemented when the preeminent drinking establishment, Benny's, became known throughout central Vermont for its cheap beer, frequent skirmishes, and the No Weapons sign prominently displayed in its front window. After a period of offering family films, the single-screen movie theater returned to profitability by displaying X-rated reels. (True to the sort of delicious irony and self-deprecating humor that infuses Hardwick, the spot where the theater was located is now a "peace park.")

But even as Hardwick's economy entered a period of decline due to the flows of stone and cash subsiding, something else began to take root: Scores of French Canadians began arriving in Hardwick and settling on the fertile farmland surrounding the town. This started in about 1915, not long after the Industrial Revolution lured dozens of Hardwick–area farmers to the plentiful and lucrative manufacturing jobs in the cities, leaving thousands of acres fallow. Sheep had been the primary crop, but now many of the farms were abandoned, the houses slowly melting into the ground, the pastures slowly reverting to forest, everything returning to the rich soil. Meanwhile, a couple hundred miles to the north, Quebecois farmers struggled to overcome the stony soils that define the eastern expanse of Canada. It didn't take long for the obvious to happen.

Agriculture came to Hardwick in a big way. Bellevance, LeCours, Demers, Fontaine, Broucheaux: Many of the town's farms were bought by French Canadian dairy farmers for $10 or $20 an acre. They had large families—8, 10, even 15 children—and worked relentlessly hard: milking, haying, sugaring, logging. Spring, summer, fall, winter, 7 days per week, 4 weeks per month, 12 months per year. Always working. Many of them settled along Center Road, a six-mile, ridge-top stretch that connects Hardwick and Greensboro. At one point, there were nearly a dozen farms along Center Road, and the majority were owned and operated by immigrants from the north.

The influx of French Canadians and the agricultural industry they helped create surely softened the economic blow dealt by the demise of the granite trade, and for a time, Hardwick became a base of commerce, largely supported by the farmers and their many offspring. There were clothing retailers for men and women, a jeweler, a cutler, even a photography outfit where farm families might gather for an annual portrait. There was a soda pop factory and a wood-furnace manufacturer. The Great Depression did not spare the town, but relative to many US communities during the '30s, Hardwick did pretty darn well. As a rural town with its inhabitants' values built on soil and toil, it wasn't the sort of place that had fostered speculative investing, and by today's standards (indeed, even by the standards of its day), its economy was localized. Some stores still took produce in trade for hard goods, and almost everybody had big gardens full of cucumbers, tomatoes, and sweet corn. You could buy a pair of pants, a gun, a watch, or a woodstove in town, and in the rural America of the early 1900s, there wasn't much else you needed. There were tough times in Hardwick, to be sure, but there didn't seem to be the sort of desperation that persisted in many communities of the day.

Eventually, Hardwick's dairy farms went the way of dairy farms throughout the state, dropping out of business one after another, selling the animals and equipment at auction. This started in the '50s, but didn't really hit its stride until a decade later, as milk prices stagnated, feed prices rose, and the children of those big families sought fortunes that didn't involve twice-a-day milking and 12-hour stretches of haying under a scorching July sun. Compounding the problem was that many of Hardwick's dairy farmers had reached the age when 14-hour workdays, 7 days per week, 52 weeks per year had become untenable. And they had little money; rather than contributing to retirement funds, they'd put everything into their land, buildings, and livestock. In this sense, they were wealthy, but it was another generation's definition of wealth, and as their bodies rebelled against the day-in, day-out labor of running a dairy farm and their children turned their backs on the farming life, they had little choice but to sell.

If there was a silver lining in the demise of Hardwick's family-run dairy industry, it was this: The spate of farm dissolution coincided with the antiestablishment, back-to-the-land movement of the late '60s and '70s. Hardwick, with its remoteness, pastoral beauty, and suddenly agreeably priced farmland, became something of a hippie beacon. To many, the town had become a place to get away from it all, to find a few acres and build a little house out of salvaged lumber and windows and create a life that was quieter and more connected to the natural world than the one they'd left behind. They'd grow some carrots. Potatoes. Kale. Maybe keep a few goats or a flock of chickens. Confirmation of the movement came in 1975, when the Buffalo Mountain Food Cooperative opened in town; like all good food cooperatives, it was small and funky, but it served the critical purpose of providing Hardwick's new generation of farmers with a market for their produce and goat cheese. Things continued more or less in this vein for nearly three decades. The town wasn't flourishing, exactly: For many residents, times were still hard. Incomes remained depressed; unemployment was still elevated. But in a quiet, unassuming way, Hardwick seemed to have found some footing, and its image softened a bit.

The notorious bar, Benny's, closed in the mid-'90s, and although the self-deprecating jokes remained in play (How do you know the toothbrush was invented in Hardwick? Because otherwise, it'd be called the teethbrush), the town seemed to have attained a cozy level of self-assurance and pride.

The town of Hardwick, Vermont, is not immune to the effects of an industrial food system run amuck. There is a Grand Union supermarket in town; somewhat ironically, it is located almost directly across the street from the weekly farmers' market. And while both do a brisk business, there's no contest when it comes to scale. Despite the very real and tremendously important inroads made by the producers in the region, the majority of the population still depends on supermarket shelves stacked high with anonymous foods picked and processed by anonymous hands somewhere far away. With their below-the-state-average incomes, Hardwick's residents feel the pinch of food-price inflation more than most, and they suffer the physical woes associated with diets stoked by cheap and excessive calories. Diabetes, heart disease, and the multitude of woes that are directly linked to diet do not check themselves at the town line. The town's rapidly evolving food system, as ambitious and comprehensive as it is, still has many mouths and wallets to reach.

It is probably too simplistic and melodramatic to say that our nation's food system is on the verge of outright collapse. But for reasons I've already articulated, it is by no means a stretch of the imagination to suggest that things are changing, and that if we don't change with them, collapse will happen. That is why the stakes for Hardwick's food endeavor could not be higher, and not merely for the town's 3,200 citizens. While it's tempting to point at the town's ragged economy and make grand proclamations about the positive impact a regionalized food economy is beginning to have, I'd argue that even before the surge in ag-based jobs, Hardwick was better prepared to handle the challenges that are coming to confront us all. This is a town of modest means and similarly modest expectations. If circumstances force its residents to reconsider the path they're on, I believe they'll do what they've always done: Put their shoulders to the wheel and carry on.

That's not to say that the transition from globalized to localized food production and distribution will be easy. It won't. It will be deeply difficult, particularly if global events continue to unfold in such rapid, unpredictable fashion. Because we're not talking about televisions or automobiles or even electricity; we're not talking about iPods or hip-hop. These are things we can do without, however much we prefer to have them around. But *food*? This isn't about entertainment. This isn't about transportation or convenience. This is about *survival*.

One more thing: As you read this book, you might notice a distinct absence of the word "sustainable." There's a reason for this. "Sustainable," like "green" and "organic," is an easily corruptible concept that, not surprisingly, has been willfully corrupted by people who would very much like to sell you a hybrid SUV or an Energy Star–rated flat-screen TV with no money down and zero percent interest for 60 months. There is very little about agriculture that is truly sustainable. At its core, agriculture is a human manipulation of a natural process. Is there a version of agriculture that is truly sustainable? Probably so. Is there a version of agriculture that is truly sustainable *and* able to feed 7 billion people? Almost certainly not.

This is not to suggest that we must all become hunter-gatherers or, conversely, that we should simply throw down our shovels and hoes in defeat. Indeed, unless we're willing to accept a world where an even larger segment of the population is allowed to starve than is now, we must have agriculture. And because we must have agriculture, it behooves us to ensure the continued productivity of those practices, which means we must move urgently in the direction of lower-impact, low-input food production and distribution. But let's not pervert a definition by calling it "sustainable." Let's just call it what it is: a desperately needed step in the right direction.

I named this book *The Town That Food Saved* because I was smitten with the notion of a browbeaten town being raised from the metaphorical ashes on the back of food. But there is a bigger story at play, and it is a story that has implications for us all. Because, as industrial agriculture continues to fracture, it isn't merely one little town that's at risk, it is an entire model of nourishment. And so I cannot help but wonder: Could this be the town that saves food? Which, if you think about it, really means this: *Could this be the town that saves us?*

On a sun-washed Vermont hillside on a late-July afternoon with my face tilted into the day's fading heat, I stood and listened to Tom Stearns as he expounded on the woes of modern agriculture. "Who's the biggest user of energy? Agriculture! Who's the biggest user of land? Agriculture! Who's the biggest user of water? Agriculture! Who's the biggest polluter? Agriculture!" He stabbed a finger in the air for emphasis. "All we have are models of broken plans to look at. Totally, completely broken." He sipped his beer and turned to face me squarely. "In 5 years, we will have people from all over the planet visiting Hardwick to see what a healthy food system looks like."

Tom and I were standing on the sprawling hillside lawn of Heartbeet Lifesharing, a residential farming community for special-needs adults who participate in all aspects of farm operations on the sloping 160 acres of field and forest. There were drumming and a bonfire and small children running across the sunlit lawn clutching rabbits to their chests. A small herd of cows grazed on a pasture below the house, casting long shadows in the late-afternoon light. Earlier in the day, there'd been a collective effort to construct a wood-fired stone-and-clay oven, and now it sat drying, at once lumpen and graceful. If one were looking for an inspiring setting in which to discuss localized agriculture, with all its ancillary benefits of social good and pastoral beauty, one couldn't have imagined a better stage.

Over the past months and years, there's been a lot of this sort of discussion in Hardwick. And lately, Tom Stearns, the owner of a seed company called High Mowing Organic Seeds, had found himself thrust (or was he thrusting himself?) into the spotlight with increasing frequency before audiences that seemed only to grow in size. He talked about America's industrial food system and how it had become frayed and vulnerable, how it sucked the sweet life out of our nation's towns and cities and out of the bodies and minds of the people who lived in these communities. He talked about the dangers of our dependence on this system, on the urgent need to wean ourselves from its power, to develop an antidote to its multitudinous ills. He spoke of the social good that would arise from making this seismic shift in how we feed ourselves. But mostly, he talked about this little town that was embarking on an ambitious quest to define itself as the community that would show the rest of America what a healthy, functioning—and okay, maybe even sustainable—food system might look like, and how other communities, towns, and even cities will learn from Hardwick.

And on that halcyon summer afternoon at Heartbeet Lifesharing, as I stood in what felt like the soft center of a lush, fertile greenness that permeated everything, I listened to him unfold his vision and believed it because I could see it all laid out before me: The cows nuzzling for tufts of ripe grass, the wholesome-looking neighbors gathered to share wholesome-looking dishes (I regretted my decision to eat earlier with my family, who'd stayed home) that were surely comprised of local ingredients, the emotionally and behaviorally challenged men and women who were finding meaning and purpose in this agrarian landscape and the day-in, day-out demands of running a farm. There was nothing to argue here. There was only health and bounty and promise. This was what a food system should look like. *Of course* the world would take notice; *of course* people would come from all its corners to see this wonderful thing being created in this wonderful little town. Who could resist?

I snapped myself out of my reverie. Stearns had dropped into a rare moment of silence, fiddling with the frilly elastic hair band around his neck (he has two young daughters, who were frolicking on the lawn below us). How? I asked him. How do you create this thing? How do you break it down into little pieces; how do you address the hard questions of money and regulation and simple habits? How do you take this—I swept my arm across our view—and export it, scale it? How do you make it something that's not just for foodies, for the affluent and aware?

Stearns, in what I would come to recognize as his preferred, oratorical style, spoke in the florid language of a politician running for office. "We can export a lot of things, but I think our main gift will be inspiration." He flared his nostrils and adjusted the hair band. "We're going to be exporting a lot of inspiration." It sounded nice, though it wasn't a terribly satisfying answer. But by then, I'd finished my second beer and someone had dropped a pie onto the picnic table. The drums were beating a nice groove and I felt my hips moving. I wasn't in the mood to press the issue. Tom Stearns and I strolled across the grass toward the pie.

Perched atop that high ridge at Heartbeet Lifesharing, I was at the nexus of a small web of communities linked to Hardwick village by a few miles of weather-cracked pavement and gravel lane. To the east, there are Woodbury, Walden, and Cabot, the latter being where I make my home. All are smaller than Hardwick by a good bit, which means they're really, really damn small. To the west is Wolcott and just beyond that, Hyde Park; to the south, South Woodbury; and a couple dozen more miles down the road is the relative metropolis of Montpelier, with its 10,000 souls. To the north lie Craftsbury and Greensboro, the latter of which is situated on the shores of Lake Caspian and largely populated by well-off summer folk who arrive in June and retreat back to Connecticut or New York or New Jersey on Labor Day. Greensboro is only six or seven miles from Hardwick and yet, as is the case with my childhood home of Maple Corner, Vermont, it resides in another universe, socioeconomically speaking. In more than one way, this has proved a blessing to Hardwick, because Greensboro itself lacks much infrastructure (there is a wonderful general store along with a couple of inns, but that's about it), leaving the relatively affluent summer residents little choice but to make the short pilgrimage here for groceries and drug-store necessities.

In any case, while it's true that Hardwick serves as the heart of the region's agriculture movement and that Hardwick is the only town in the immediate vicinity with the infrastructure (modest as it is) to support such a movement, many of the businesses and people mentioned throughout this book are actually based in one of the surrounding towns. There's Jasper Hill Farm and Cheese Cellars in Greensboro, High Mowing Organic Seeds in Wolcott, Applecheek Farm in Hyde Park, and Pete's Greens in Craftsbury. Between them and the two dozen or so others I haven't yet mentioned, they labor over what could very well be, per capita, the most fertile region for artisanal food production in North America.

This is clearly intriguing, but if it's to truly become a model for other communities, there are many questions to be asked: How did this come about? Why here? Who are the protagonists, and where did they come from? What is the difference between a bunch of small-scale, artisan-quality food producers who happen to be clustered in a particular region and an honest-to-goodness reproducible model? And what of the blue-collar locals, reared on diets of cheap industrial calories? Because $20-per-pound cheese and $5-per-loaf bread are unlikely to find an easy path to their tables.

Finally, most broadly and intriguingly, we must ask the question: What should a decentralized food system look like? Clearly, there are necessary components—physical, structural, societal— but less clear is how they should interact to promote both a high degree of food security and, beyond that, communal vigor and pride. The champions of local food claim it has a laundry list of ancillary benefits: Economic stability, social and even political engagement, a working landscape preserved for generations to come. Can it really be true that something as simple as food will deliver all this? Or is it really not that simple at all?

To know if the emerging Hardwick agricultural model will truly work, we need to poke and prod and challenge it from every angle. Indeed, we need to—at least for a time—ignore the very premise that begat this book: that it's a good thing, an honorable and worthy undertaking. It may seem absurd that it might not be (and clearly, I'm predisposed to believing in it), but for now, let us cast aside our presumptions and allow the story to unfold as it will.

CHAPTER TWO

I began reporting on Hardwick's agricultural uprising in May 2008 while on assignment for *Gourmet* magazine. I certainly wasn't the first to stumble upon the story; there'd been significant local media coverage by the time I completed my article in July. But during the latter half of '08, the national media floodgates opened, most notably with a *New York Times* feature. The story ran on the front page of the paper's dining section, with color photos of many of the town's food producers proudly displaying their wares: Tomatoes. Carrots. Cabbage. Peppers. Tofu. Apple pie. Everyone and everything seemed to glow with vitality and purpose. There was also a picture of Hardwick's block-long Main Street, rain-wet and dreary looking. An old Ford pickup was rolling down the road. The title was "Uniting Around Food to Save an Ailing Town."

Indeed, the media seemed to fall in line behind the *Times*'s headline: Hardwick had been on the brink of collapse, but now, thanks to this small group of forward-thinking noblemen and noblewomen, the town would be rescued from a bleak present and an even dimmer future. There was little to no mention of the region's long-established farmers, the vibrancy of the local populace, or historical role of agriculture in Hardwick. There was no discussion of the potential pitfalls and shortcomings of this recent food-based push, or whether it was really the best articulation of a local food system.

I'm pretty sure I know why: The story of Hardwick's agricultural revolution was just so damn . . . perfect. To the enterprising freelance journalist (*c'est moi*), it presented itself as a gift, neatly wrapped in recycled paper and adorned with a big, fat biodegradable bow. A gritty town with a maligned reputation; a national, if not global, awakening that all is not right with our industrial ag system; an effusive, articulate, and absurdly colorful movement leader (Stearns) who was making bold promises. It was a great American story of redemption and pride, of a town and its people pulling themselves up by their collective bootstraps by utilizing what unites us all: food.

So I, like many others, tucked in. I met with Tom Stearns, and I joined a tour he'd organized for bank loan officers, community fund managers, and basically anyone with access to large piles of cash who might be convinced that small-scale agriculture was a good place to park it. We crammed into rented vans and were whisked from one regional producer to another. Applecheek Farm, the Cellars at Jasper Hill Farm, Vermont Soy, Claire's Restaurant and Bar, Pete's Greens, High Mowing Organic Seeds. The money people oohed and ahhed and tried not to dip their wingtips into anything that looked like mud but wasn't. I stayed mostly quiet, trying to play the role of objective journalist, but like that afternoon at Heartbeet Lifesharing, I could feel myself being drawn to the story, charmed by Stearns's unrelenting optimism and the apparent righteousness of it all. The tour was a piece of genius, really, ripe with authenticity, wholesomeness, and promise. These were real people, working real soil, and that stuff that looked like mud but wasn't? Yes indeedy, real cow shit.

Everything was so tangible: The smells of the dirt and poop; the cool damp of the cheese cave; the smooth, creamy texture of its contents; the incongruous orange of a carrot against the brown earth it'd been pulled from; the sonorous lowing of cattle. And, when viewed through a certain lens, the one colored by Hardwick's storied reputation, the town *did* appear somewhat bereft. Houses flaked paint, cars flaked rust, and two of the largest buildings in the downtown area were abandoned and needed extensive repairs. The connection between the hope and potential of the region's evolving food network and the apparent faded glory of the town felt obvious and right, and I got the sense that I had been invited to peek behind a curtain at something new and promising that was unfolding from the field-calloused hands of these hardworking young men and women. It was—oh, hell, I'll just say it—*inspirational*. I knew the story would resonate, and I couldn't wait to tell it.

It didn't take me long to determine the key players in Hardwick's agrepreneurial (a word I coined to describe the agrarian entrepreneurialism that infuses many of the region's food-based enterprises) movement or the internal dynamics that had developed. Tom Stearns had been the easiest to peg; his vast and seemingly inexhaustible enthusiasm, his enviable skill at articulating the issues, and his passion, combined with a certain degree of unselfconscious goofiness, made him the lovable Lab puppy of the bunch. When his name comes up in conversation, Stearns is one of those people about whom others exchange knowing looks and perhaps a shared remembrance of something silly.

The other Tom, Tom Gilbert, executive director of the Highfields Center for Composting, is the foil to Stearns's overwhelming exuberance. It's not that Gilbert doesn't express excitement or optimism, it's just that he does so in such a low-key, thoughtful manner that, to someone unfamiliar with his persona and not listening carefully to his words, it can masquerade as world-weary pessimism. And while Stearns is articulate in a sound-bite, layperson kind of way ("Inspiration! We'll be exporting lots of inspiration!"), Gilbert's artful use of his enormous vocabulary can at times feel impenetrable. Of all the agrepreneurs, he seemed the most willing to apply the brakes to ensure that things unfolded in a thoughtful way. This, he hoped, would ultimately lead to a level of self-reliance far beyond what most people could imagine, and he seemed to believe that the process had implications beyond the physical. "A lot of this work gets to be spiritual. We can't advance the cause without being willing to grow, and expansionism, whether it's personal or economic or social, can be a very moving and even dangerous thing." I thought maybe I knew what he meant.

Pete Johnson, founder and farmer-in-chief at Pete's Greens, with his tousled, farmer-hunk looks and constant experimentation and expansion, had assumed the role of model grower, the 21st-century answer to the question an awful lot of people seemed to be asking: What might small-scale organic farming, food production, and distribution look like? He had opinions and he'd voice them if asked, but mostly he stuck to himself and worked his ass off. Too, there was something compelling about the elemental nature of his work of coaxing food from the soil. There was no mystique or magic about it; the infrastructure was basic, logical, and by and large built according to a generations-old ethos that hard physical work isn't something to be shunned, but rather to be embraced and honored. And although some had articulated to me a belief that Johnson's operation exceeded the scale appropriate for the region, there could be little doubt that he'd probably done more to put actual food on the tables of his fellow Vermonters than almost anyone in the region. "I consider my occupation to be the highest occupation a person can have," he told me early in my reporting. It occurred to me that many more Americans might agree with this sentiment now than would have only a year or two ago, and this felt like a very hopeful thing.

Then there was Andrew Meyer. Quiet and unassuming, with a boyish, "aw, shucks" demeanor, Meyer deserved as much credit for Hardwick's recent rise to agricultural fame as anyone. The Center for an Agricultural Economy was his brainchild; he owns two of the region's most-heralded ag-based businesses; and he'd been one of the first of the agrepreneurs to start talking about Hardwick in a way that suggested that the town might someday be something more than a loose collection of folks quietly working the soil. He seemed content to have ceded the mouthpiece role to Tom Stearns, perhaps because he recognized Stearns's prodigious talent in these matters, or perhaps because he understood that administering to the press and the public scrutiny that could result required a level of focus that would not serve his business endeavors well. Or maybe it was not so calculated; maybe it was just the way things had unfolded.

Of course, there are many others involved in Hardwick's food system, some of whom have been plying their trades since before Andrew Meyer, Pete Johnson, and the Toms were out of diapers. But this was the quartet that emerged early in my reporting as champions of the agrepreneurial movement: The Mouth, the Mind, the Manager, and the Model Farmer. Seed Baron, Compost King, Soy Boy, and Field Prince. To the extent that Hardwick's food revolution is a success, these four men can claim a large share of the credit. To the extent that it is a failure, they will shoulder much of the blame. And to the extent that I was going to understand this story, not just in the gift-wrapped manner in which it originally presented itself, but in a truly honest and substantive way that assumed as little as possible and might burst my remaining assumptions and drag my inspiration through the thick mud (or something that looked like mud) of a Hardwick barnyard, these were but a few of the folks I was going to have to get to know.

CHAPTER THREE

By the time I received my contract from *Gourmet*, I'd known Tom Stearns for many years, but only from a distance. We'd both bounced around the north-central, small-scale Vermont agriculture community for a decade or more, myself almost entirely on the coattails of my wife, Penny, who managed the field crew at Cate Farm, a 22-acre organic vegetable operation outside the state capital of Montpelier, for nearly a decade. Tom had spent those same years growing his organic heirloom seed business, High Mowing Organic Seeds, into a $2-million-per-year, 30-employee enterprise. But I'd never really talked to Stearns face-to-face, and I hadn't spoken with him since he'd become engaged in the Hardwick project.

Actually, "engaged" isn't nearly a strong enough word. It took me about three minutes to decide that Stearns was obsessed by his vision. I couldn't yet tell if that obsession drives the restless energy that seems to constantly course through his wiry frame and long, angular face or if the restless energy drives the obsession. In either case, the energy presents itself in his voice; he speaks loudly, running through his self-prescribed talking points fluidly and often. And it presents itself in his physical bearing, the way he uses his hands to punctuate his speech and his habit of scrunching his nose to halt the slide of his wire-rim eyeglasses, which flares his nostrils and makes him look momentarily unhinged. He laughs easily, loudly, and somewhat girlishly and stops talking just often enough to avoid appearing self-centered. He is one of those people who seem comfortable in their bodies, and he asks thoughtful questions, even when the focus is on him. Whether he does this because he's genuinely curious or because he knows it's endearing I couldn't immediately tell. In simple terms, he has the gift of gab. These were my first impressions.

Tom Stearns was born in Sherman, Connecticut, in 1975. He has two sisters, both older than he is. His father, Peter, was a classical music composer; his mother, Marcia, was also a composer and ran a small press that published sacred music. She was also deeply involved in community development, particularly with the significant population of refugees from Southeast Asia that settled into the region during the '70s.

The Stearnses weren't farmers, per se, but they did keep large gardens and Peter was a committed nature lover. "I remember my dad would wake us up at four in the morning to watch deer. And he'd do stuff like secretly plant rings of daffodil bulbs out in the woods. Then he'd take us out there and pretend to be surprised. All us kids thought it was fairy magic."

Tom believes that his father's affinity for nature and wonderment is the product of his unusual schooling. When Peter was four, his father died; not long after, Peter was sent to a farm-based boarding school. This was in Los Angeles in the 1940s. "The guy who ran the place was adamant about the benefits of raw milk," Tom told me. "He was teaching the kids how to build compost piles with seaweed and manure, and they were doing all these pagan celebrations to mark the seasons." He was also a follower of Madame Blavatsky, who founded the Theosophical Society in 1875 after suffering a limb-threatening leg infection. Blavatsky treated the infection by having a white dog sleep across the ailing appendage each night, and while she recuperated she began to imagine a way of thinking that fused Eastern spiritual knowledge with the hard, reality-based world of new science.

Blavatsky died in 1891, but her influence continued to be felt through a number of esoteric thinkers of the time, including Rudolf Steiner. Steiner founded the Waldorf educational system and developed a method of agriculture known as biodynamic farming, which views farms as unified organisms, with interrelated soil, plants, and animals in a closed, self-nourishing system. Biodynamic farmers tend to be fervent believers in raw milk, compost, trace minerals, and astrological influences on crops and animals, and they do things like bury manure-filled cow horns in the autumn. The manure is left to decompose until spring, at which point it is dug up; a teaspoonful of the composted cow shit is removed, dumped into a dozen gallons of water, and stirred for a full hour, changing the direction every minute. In biodynamic circles, this mixture is known as 500, and it is added to field soil to increase the microfloral, nutrient, and trace element content. (There are a total of nine biodynamic preparations that utilize similar ingredients and exacting techniques.)

In any event, Peter Stearns was deeply affected by the teachings of his headmaster, and that influence trickled down to his son. "My dad had us making compost piles when I was 10," recalls Stearns, who sends his girls to a Waldorf school. "And believe it or not, I thought it was pretty damn cool."

The sway of agriculture on Tom Stearns's life only deepened during his teen years, when he attended Northfield Mount Hermon, a private school in the rural, north-central Massachusetts town of Gill. At Northfield Mount Hermon, students construct all the campus buildings and, as a mandatory portion of whatever study program they choose, run a diversified vegetable and livestock farm that includes a 2,000-tap maple-syrup operation.

Stearns ended up at Arizona's Prescott College after implementing and overseeing a recycling program on a Hopi reservation. At Prescott, he double-majored in agriculture and community development; in his senior year, as part of a self-designed, off-campus study program, he wandered back east to his sister's farm in Bedford, Pennsylvania. And, at the age of 19, he started growing seed. "I love seeds," he told me. "What else can you put in your pocket, walk 500 miles, and [use to] start a village?"

Because all plants produce seed and all seed comes from plants (this might sound painfully obvious, but in Stearns's experience, few people actually grasp the genesis of seed), raising seed demands basically the same skills as growing a garden; you simply allow it to grow longer, until the plant has flowered and the seed has reached maturity. This is often—but not always—beyond the point of palatability.

I'd never considered the vastness of the seed industry (which globally is worth nearly $43 billion annually) or its essential role in almost every facet of our lives. When I mentioned this to Tom, he nodded his head crisply. "Look at that shirt you're wearing." (A faded flannel from L.L. Bean, a gift from my father many Christmases ago.) "Cotton, right? Where do you think cotton comes from?" It was a rhetorical question, and like many rhetorical questions, it was posed to make a point: Even our modern, digitized, information economy cannot overcome the importance of the humble seed. Without seed, our economy would not exist, because without seed, food would not exist. Without seed, *we* would not exist.

Stearns's seed-saving habit, which he picked up while at his sister's farm, soon blossomed into a business, and he launched High Mowing Organic Seeds, a production and retail outfit that specializes in organically tended, heirloom varieties. By this time, he'd moved to Vermont and rented a farm in Holland, a rural town tight against the Canadian border. He lived as a bachelor farmer, lonely but for the company of his sheep, a milk cow named Posey, chickens, and hogs. "It was just me, my dog, Posey, and my truck. I was selling meat, eggs, animals, and seeds," he says. To pass the time, he taught himself how to armpit fart ("I'm very, very good; I'll play for you sometime") and he taught his dog, Rowan, to hump inanimate objects on command. That year, he made about $10,000, and he must have realized that he was at high risk of becoming a poverty-stricken, eccentric country hick. He considered his options, which seemed to fall into three categories: stick it out in Holland, go on the road with Rowan and his musical armpit, or specialize. "I decided to put my efforts into seeds pretty quick." He found a cheap piece of property in Wolcott that included an old trailer home and in 1999, he moved himself and his nascent business.

High Mowing's business model is unique in an industry that has traditionally been split between global wholesale producers who sell bulk seed to retailers, some of whom specialize in the industrial farm market (certainly the path for the seeds that grew the cotton that became my shirt), some of whom specialize in the commercial vegetable market, and some of whom court the home gardener. High Mowing does buy some seed from wholesalers, but the bulk of its seed is produced by independent contractors who have been supplied with stock the company has developed in one of its trial gardens. About a third of these producers are in Vermont; the remainder are scattered across the world. (Some of High Mowing's seeds are produced in Israel.) According to Stearns, this arrangement allows High Mowing an unmatched ability to offer and experiment with, as Stearns puts it, "obscure New England heirloom shit. If you're a $50 million wholesale-seed producer, you're not going to grow something unless you perceive a huge market. We can afford to grow something just because we think it might be fun."

Fun is clearly a motivating factor in Stearns's choice of occupation, but he's keenly aware that in a world dependent on a handful of seed companies offering a handful of varieties to a broken agricultural model, his work has implications beyond cultivating the obscure for shits and giggles. "The problem is, we've got a seed industry that's basically encouraging bad farming." He was talking about the recent proliferation of genetically modified organisms (GMOs), which have gained firm footing in the world of seed technology by companies seeking to create plants that are resistant to drought, pests, disease, and chemical weed killers. These sound like noble pursuits, but Stearns sees it as a crude bandage applied to an agricultural system that's rapidly painting itself into a corner: "You farm badly, so the soil gets salinated and won't grow anything, so you come up with something in the lab to accommodate all the salt, and now you've got a crop that has to be irrigated, which only wicks more salt to the topsoil. . . . God, it's just a vicious cycle, and the presence of GMOs just supports and expands it," Stearns sighed. We were speaking on the phone, so I couldn't see his face, but he sounded as weary as I'd ever heard him.

There's another problem with genetically modified seed: The technology allows for the production of so-called terminator technology. These are seeds that have been tweaked to render their crops sterile. Terminator technology denies farmers the option of saving seed from year to year. If the practice of seed-saving sounds like a quaint throwback to another generation, consider this: 90 percent of the wheat seed sown by Canadian wheat farmers is saved from the previous year's crop. And that's just one industry in one country.

Rather conveniently for the seed producer, terminator seed makes growers dependent on their product year in and year out. The technology has yet to be commercialized; in 1999, Monsanto, which owns the patent, responded to public outcry by committing to keep terminator seeds under wraps. But a statement upholding the company's right to commercially develop terminator technology in the future tempered that commitment.

Gloomy as all this is to anyone who cares about society's ability and right to feed itself, it must be exponentially more depressing to the founder of an organic heirloom-seed business that holds free seed-saving workshops, essentially teaching its customers how to never have to purchase its seed again. Still, as I was beginning to learn, Tom Stearns's life view is predicated on seeking out silver linings, and his tone quickly brightened. "GMOs have done more to educate people on cross-pollinating, contamination, and seeds in general. Yes, they're a waste of time and energy and resources, but the whole issue has made people think about seeds. You'd be amazed how many people don't think about seeds, ever." Actually, I was more amazed that Stearns assumed I'd be shocked that the majority of Americans don't think about seeds on a regular basis.

Because of his energy, charm, and drive, Stearns has become the de facto mouthpiece for Hardwick's rapidly evolving food scene, a role that fits neatly into a suitcase of ag- and business-related titles he carries: president of High Mowing Organic Seeds, board copresident of the Northeast Organic Farming Association Vermont chapter, ambassador for Vermont Businesses for Social Responsibility, founding member and advisory board member for Slow Money USA, board member Vermont Vegetable and Berry Growers Association. Most recently, he was named president of the Center for an Agricultural Economy. By the time you read this, the list will probably be longer.

Tom Stearns, his wife, Heather, and their two daughters, Cora and Ruby, don't actually live in Hardwick; Wolcott is one village west, about 10 miles down Route 15. High Mowing's offices and warehouse are located in Wolcott; Stearns sleeps, works, pays taxes, and votes in Wolcott. But with Hardwick becoming ground zero for the local agriculture movement, and with every fiber of his being compelling him to promote that movement, Stearns has aligned himself with a town that's not officially his own. His face and quotes appear regularly in the *Hardwick Gazette*, and he often can be found at the bar in the back of Claire's, pressing flesh and tipping pints like a politician running for office. When he talks about food systems, he talks about Hardwick's food system, and when he thinks about his future, he thinks about it mostly as it relates to Hardwick. The town's fortunes and his own have become all but inseparable. There is a degree of controversy surrounding Stearns's ambition for Hardwick, its food system, and its people, but this controversy seems not to have much to do with the fact that he doesn't even live there. If he were from Montpelier or, worse yet, Massachusetts, it would be an issue. But like Hardwick, Wolcott is small, self-reliant, and a bit rough around the edges. It is a sister town by geography, sociology, and economy, and therefore the community tensions bubbling up around Tom Stearns and his aspirations don't have anything to do with the fact that he is, strictly speaking, an outsider, if only by a handful of miles. Indeed, they run deeper than that.

CHAPTER FOUR

My interest in the story of Hardwick, Vermont, hangs on more than my desire to score a plum magazine assignment. As I already mentioned, I grew up in the region. I knew Hardwick's back story, or at least its broad strokes. I'd shopped at the Buffalo Mountain Food Co-op with my mother back in the late '70s and early '80s, not long after we'd moved from the rural northwestern reaches of Vermont to Maple Corner. Up north, we'd lived in a two-room cabin perched at the upper edge of a sloping field, part of the 160 acres my father had bought in the late '60s for $15,000. In the simplest terms, my parents had been homesteaders and hippies; they'd kept chickens and a garden, and the cabin featured neither electricity nor running water. My dad was a poet, my mom milked cows at a farm down the road, and like all good hippie children, I spent my days naked and dirty.

But my agricultural roots run deeper than the rocky gardens my parents tended, or the two pigs they raised one summer (a gift from my Uncle Kent, exactly the sort of fellow who'd show up at his brother's home for a surprise visit with a pair of piglets in the trunk of his car), or the flock of laying hens I recall only for the sight of my father sprinting, naked, .22-caliber rifle in hand, to the coop to defend the family against a hungry raccoon. I used to think I'd imagined this, but alas, I did not.

My mother had been raised on a farm in southeastern Iowa, a stone's throw from the borders of Illinois and Missouri on 300 acres of fertile bottomland devoted to corn, soybeans, and beef cattle. Back in those days, it was a decent-size farm, an "industrial" farm if you will, or at least an early, quaint version of one. But it was still dependent on chemical fertilizers, large machinery, and the vagaries of the commodities market.

If I appreciated the farm as a child, it was only for the tractor rides my grandfather granted during our annual visits. I particularly loved the combine, its cab so high we had to climb a ladder to find our seats, its view so expansive a little boy could imagine the world ended where the sky and earth met on the other side of those vast fields. My grandfather wasn't a talkative fellow; he didn't so much converse as offer single-syllable commentary on the matter at hand. So we pretty much just sat in the combine, listening to the radio and the constant rumble of the big diesel engine, watching the cornstalks fall in waves before us.

If there was any agricultural imprinting taking place, I was not aware of it. My grandparents weren't the sort of farmers who articulated their ties to the land or their passion for the hard work that defined their days. Maybe that's because they didn't feel these things, though I doubt it: One doesn't spend one's entire life working the same square of soil if one doesn't *feel* it. How many times must my grandfather have driven that combine over the same piece of ground? How many head of cattle must he have loaded into a livestock trailer to make the long journey to the stockyards in Chicago? How many hours must he have spent listening to the commodity reports on the radio, wondering whether to sell and take the beating or hold and hope for better prices? These things, so mundane and repetitive, must have been part of something bigger and more forceful that compelled him to keep doing them. If my grandfather ever thought about these things, he didn't share them with me. Or maybe it was simply this: He had never known anything else. He'd been raised on a farm, he'd become a farmer, he'd stayed a farmer, he'd died a farmer. Is it possible that when something defines your life from birth to death, you lack a certain context necessary to appreciate its subtleties? Yes, I think that's possible.

I'm glad he shared his combine. In fact, now that I think about it, perhaps that was the best thing he could have done: At seven years of age, I was not going to appreciate the deeper, soulful layers of his life's work. But a ride in a combine, with the cornstalks bowing neatly before us, with my grandfather probably unsure of what to say or how to say it but thoughtful enough to allow me to put a small hand on the steering wheel, at least for a moment or two? That, I could appreciate. That, I could understand.

So I found myself being drawn to farming, or to something like it. I married a girl who'd left the Rochester Institute of Technology, in New York, one semester short of a photography degree so she could work on a farm. She'd been reared in the New Jersey suburbs; her dad was a dentist and her brother went to business school. She wanted to dig in the dirt. And with that girl, I bought 40 acres in the town of Cabot, Vermont, a property we chose because it was the only one we could find in our price range that offered enough open land to keep some animals and turn over a garden or two. Today, I can look up from my work to see our three cows grazing the remnants of summer grass through a thin skim of snow. I can see our hundred blueberry bushes, which last August became so thick with fruit we lost a few branches to the weight. I can see the "wedding garden," so named because it sits on one of the few flat spots of our land, which is why we put our wedding tent there the summer we got married.

We don't make our living as farmers; in a typical year, we might sell a side or two of beef, a few hundred quarts of blueberries, and a couple of pigs. It doesn't amount to much, maybe a couple thousand dollars a year, which, once expenses are deducted, nets us a gross profit of perhaps a hundred bucks. I say "maybe" because I really don't know; we don't track our farm-related finances with anything but the most rudimentary, back-of-a-napkin calculations. And we don't account for our labor, in part because it doesn't feel like labor to us, but also because the harsh truth of how much we're actually getting paid to haul hay, shovel shit, and chase marauding pigs through the woods might convince us to do something rational—which would surely mean the end of our little farm-based enterprise.

So maybe what we do is irrational or, at the very least, defies conventional logic. Our neighbor, who has milked cows his entire life and currently keeps about 60 head with his eldest son, calls us "wannabe farmers." This is not said unkindly and although I used to find it vaguely offensive, I've come to accept it as the truth. And also as nothing to be ashamed of. What could be wrong with wanting to farm? What could be wrong with wanting it enough that not even the reasonable and rational can dissuade you?

All the while, Hardwick has existed on the periphery of my life. After we settled in Cabot in 1998, it slowly became our destination for anything we couldn't find in our own town, which has a fantastic hardware store, a wonderful library, a garage, a post office, a diner, and a well-stocked village grocery, but not much more. We became regulars at the Buffalo Mountain Food Co-op and, after I bought an old Ford tractor at Rowell Brothers, the tractor-repair-and-supply shop. When I learned to slaughter our livestock, I went to Rite Way Sports, just down the road from the co-op, and bought a gun. A couple years later, when my oldest son, Finlay, became obsessed with fishing, I picked up a couple of fishing poles. When I came down with a bacterial sinus infection that wouldn't subside, I filled my prescription in Hardwick. Every so often, we buy a book at the Galaxy Bookshop, though mostly we visit the Cabot library for our literary excursions.

Hardwick doesn't have much of a business district, but it's enough to meet our needs. Maybe that's in part because we've tailored our expectations to the town's infrastructure: If we can't find it in Hardwick, the logic goes, we probably don't need it. I don't think we're the only ones who loosely follow this rule. In fact, I'm certain we're not. Sure, there are plenty of things you *can't* find in Hardwick—there's no movie theater, no electronics store, no place to get a new pair of boots or a bedside table—but you could go months without needing anything more than the town can provide. In this way, I like to think that the town keeps us honest in our role as consumers. At the very least, it cuts down on my impulse purchases, as long as I restrain from picking up handguns and tractor tires on a whim.

So a large part of my interest in Hardwick's evolving food system was based on the simple fact that it has the potential to impact my life on a day-to-day basis. How might the town change in the face of this evolution? How would my interactions with the town shift? Could Hardwick's character survive the spotlight of these new ambitions? And was that a bigger, more important issue than the impact on its economy? The broader local food movement had always seemed to me like an abstraction and a luxury for those with the time (and by default, the money) to ponder the carbon footprint of their milk and meatballs. The juxtaposition between the overt "blue-collarness" of Hardwick and my perception of local food as a precious, upscale concern fascinated me.

Then came the creeping awareness that my take on the local food movement was naive; that no place, no class, no one could afford to ignore the issue any longer. Credit that awareness to writers such as Michael Pollan and fellow Vermonter Bill McKibben, who foretold much that occurred in the latter half of 2007 and early 2008: the sudden, sharp uptick in food prices and the seeping understanding that all was not well in the breadbasket of our nation. To me, there was no small amount of irony in the notion that Hardwick—humble, rough 'n' tumble Hardwick—could be a tonic to these ills. It wasn't that I didn't believe in the town or what was happening; it was just too hard to imagine anyone paying much attention to the place. After all, for nearly a century, since the region was a granite hotbed, they hadn't. Why would they now?

Maybe because the media recognized the urgency. More cynically, maybe they imagined the same story line I had: a trendy movement bringing salvation to a hard town. It seemed an obvious and easy story, without the complications of controversy or the need for any measure of true, investigative journalism.

But the more I thought about what was happening in Hardwick and mulled over the enormity of the issues facing our national food system, the more questions I had. They weren't complicated questions, but it seemed to me that they'd largely been ignored in the media rush on Hardwick and the national discourse surrounding local food. Most basic was this: What should a decentralized food system look like? The young, entrepreneurial protagonists of what was evolving in Hardwick claimed they were going to blueprint the process and the product, offering it for export to other communities. A noble undertaking, to be sure. But did they really know how to build such a system, much less dissect its building blocks for mass consumption? I was coming to feel as if I'd been seduced by a notion without really understanding how it would work. What defines this thing? What are the specific components? What makes it work? What might make it fail? Because frankly, without any context, it's just a nice idea, an amorphous and shifting ideal. The industrial food system hijacked "organic" by applying it to foods that are grown in adherence to a strict set of federal guidelines. Those guidelines might be well and good, but there's an awful lot that happens beyond them that has made a mockery of the organic movement. Could the same thing happen to the local food movement? I didn't know. And what of the claims put forward by these ambitious Hardwick agriculturalists and numerous other food system and economic thinkers—that local foods can rebuild communities, economies, souls? It seemed so compelling, so simple, so *right.* But was it true? I didn't know, but if I wanted to learn, Hardwick would be the ideal classroom.

Then there are the people. Some, like Tom Stearns, I knew. Some, like the organic vegetable farmer who'd flown helicopters in Vietnam, worked as a roadie for Grand Funk Railroad, and, at the age of 60, still drives to the New Hampshire coast every few weeks to go surfing, I knew of. Every small town has its characters, and every one of these characters has a story. The fact that these just might be the people to show us the way out of the agricultural morass we're in provided me with the welcome excuse I needed to invade their lives.

A story that had started as an obvious extension of my place in life, physically, historically, and practically, had become an exercise in thought and process that, for a period of my life, consumed nearly all my waking hours. I talked about it with my wife, my kids, my friends, and anyone who would listen. Sometimes, usually as I went about the daily tasks of a small farm, I talked about it with myself. If the cows heard or held an opinion, they never said. I talked about it so much because I truly felt—and still do—that it was enormously important, that the questions I was grappling with will soon become part of our national conversation on a scale and with an urgency we can hardly imagine.

CHAPTER FIVE

Not long after my visit with Tom Stearns at Heartbeet Lifesharing, I awoke in the predawn hours to face an uncomfortable truth I'd thus far failed to acknowledge: *I didn't know what I was looking for.* Part of this acceptance was based on an unreasonable expectation that Stearns would have the answers to all my questions. There had been much recent talk about local food systems in Hardwick and among a segment of the national population, most of whom had read Michael Pollan's *The Omnivore's Dilemma* and had found their world—or at least the portion of their world that revolves around food—turned upside down. That local food was noble, healthy, and something to strive for had become axiomatic, and I simply assumed that Tom Stearns was among the multitudes of people smarter than myself who had blessed the issue with their full attention and would be able to explain—in clear, concise terms I could grapple with—how to return our food system to vitality.

Actually, to a degree, that is what's happening in Hardwick. Or, more precisely, it's what's being attempted. And to be sure, I'd already seen signs of what seemed like rousing success. At Heartbeet Lifesharing, while chatting with Tom Stearns on that lustrous July afternoon, I'd had a vision of what a local food system could be, or at least part of what it could be, and some of what it could do. Maybe I couldn't articulate it perfectly, maybe I couldn't identify every little piece that made the puzzle come together, and perhaps I hadn't considered how it fit into the community as a whole, but I knew it was *right*.

But feeling that something is right and identifying *why* it's right are two very different things. In Hardwick, the challenge of the latter was compounded by the fact that things were happening so incredibly fast. In barely three years, the town had emerged from a cocoon of relative anonymity to carry the weight of so many expectations. Every few days, I'd get an e-mail from Stearns that made it clear that it wasn't merely the people of Hardwick who expected something: The Center for an Agricultural Economy (CAE) was partnering with the University of Vermont for research and outreach on local food systems. Stearns and Meyer were scheduled to travel to Ireland on an agricultural trade mission with Vermont senator Patrick Leahy. They might have dinner with Bono. The CAE had closed on a 15-acre parcel of river bottomland in Hardwick and would construct what was being called an "eco-agricultural industrial park." The Vermont Food Venture Center, a shared-use kitchen incubator that allows private producers to create, package, and distribute specialty food products without the daunting financial commitment of constructing an on-site kitchen, would relocate to Hardwick. Global warming activist and author Bill McKibben was coming to town. A major music producer who was rumored to have worked with the Rolling Stones and Lionel Richie had heard about Hardwick, was coming to town and wanted to take "every farmer in town" to dinner at Claire's. The former head of Bear Stearns was coming for a tour. Michael Pollan might come to town, if his publisher's terms could be met. A television film crew was coming to town. A documentary movie film crew was coming to town. Dan Rather's film crew was coming to town. At any moment, I expected to hear that Stearns had been invited to appear on *Oprah* or named *People* magazine's "sexiest man of the year."

And yet, as far as I could tell, there wasn't even a metric by which to measure the progress in Hardwick's ag sector. Clearly, there was common agreement that the US food system was ailing. And clearly, there was common agreement that decentralized food systems were the tonic. But despite the recent flurry of activity in town, everything beyond that felt a little abstract and amorphous.

The goal itself seemed obvious: Stearns had repeatedly described it as "developing the wider Hardwick area as a model of a 21st-century food system," which sounded a little clunky and contrived to my ears, but was hard to argue with. And Meyer had used the phrase "establishing a healthy food system." I liked that better, although on an intuitive level, I felt like I knew what both of them meant. I mean, how can you hear someone talk about establishing a healthy food system and not nod in agreement? It's the agricultural equivalent of saving baby seals.

But how obvious was it, really? Because when you hold it up to the harsh light of critique, "establishing a healthy food system" doesn't really say a hell of a lot. It's like saying "I'm going to be a better person." It sounds good; it very well may *be* good. What I questioned was whether it was enough to reinvent the way we grow, distribute, and consume food. And whether it was even possible to overthrow an industrial food system worth nearly $1 trillion annually in the United States alone. Imagine the business interests stacked up behind a trillion dollars' worth of annual revenue. It occurred to me that "establishing a healthy food system" wasn't going to be enough to wrest a measurable fraction of this dough from their clutches.

If Stearns and Meyer didn't yet have the specifics of a healthy decentralized food system nailed down, I figured the least I could do was try to pin them down for myself. Here's what I came up with.

1. It must offer economic viability to small-scale food producers.

In the mid-1800s, 90 percent of the US population lived on farms. A century later, that figure had fallen to 37 percent. Today, it sits at about 0.7 percent. Think about that for a second: 140 of us eat what

1 of us grows. If that doesn't amaze you, it's only because you've
never tried to grow enough food for just one person, let alone 139
others. And that single farmer isn't merely keeping pace with his 90
ancestors; he's outproducing them by a wide margin. The number of
calories available to Americans, per capita, has climbed from 3,200
per day in 1980 to nearly 3,900 today. You might think this steep rise
in caloric production would have generated a food glut, and you'd be
right. But rather than feed those calories to people who are genuinely
hungry, we've feasted like starving rats, creating a host of epidemics
that are all directly linked to our profligate consumption of cheap
food. Heart disease. Diabetes. Obesity. Some cancers. And probably
a few things we haven't figured out yet. Indeed, in the United States,
diet-related disease has been linked to 70 percent of all deaths.

Such are the consequences of noshing at least 25 percent more
calories than the average person needs to maintain a healthy body
weight. And here's the shocking thing: We want more. In 2008, for
the first time ever, we ate more than we could produce. If there's a
silver lining to our agricultural predicament, it's this: Most of us
would be better off if there were *less* food around.

There are many reasons for the stunning increase in US food
production: chemical fertilizers, machinery, mechanized processing, hybridized and genetically modified seeds that tolerate
drought, pesticides, herbicides, and simple crowding (one of the
major advances in food production is a genetic manipulation of
crops that allows them to be sown closer together). It all adds up to
a massive—but almost surely temporary—increase in the carrying
capacity of an acre of farmland. In 1930, a farmer counted his bless-
ings if he could reap 20 bushels of corn per acre; in 2004, the average was 160.4 bushels per acre, with some regions clocking in at
well over 200 bushels. Predictions for 300-bushel corn are ram-
pant, perhaps as soon as 2030. Meanwhile, the average farm has
almost tripled in size, from 157 acres in 1930 to nearly 450 today.

What has this done to small-scale producers? From a financial perspective, nothing good. The economy of scale that applies to almost everything in our economy, from building cars to raising houses to serving cheeseburgers, also applies to farming. It is simply not possible to compete in a commodity market without scale and without embracing the sort of technology that can generate 200-bushel corn. My grandparents' 300-acre farm, huge in its day, would now be considered a quaint reminder of how things used to be. "Get big or get out" has become the prevailing mantra, and when you live in a nation where fewer than 1 percent of us can provide what more than 37 percent of us produced only 60 years ago, there's only room for so many. What's next? One farmer in 200? One in 500? Every step toward diluting the farming population among us is another step toward food insecurity.

If small-scale, local producers can't compete with the big dogs, how do they compete? Largely by offering "value-added" products. This is ag-speak for turning a commodity into a specialty or, as the vernacular seems to be tipping, "artisanal" product. Milk, which sells for maybe $4 per gallon, becomes yogurt, which fetches three times that. Beef stays beef (it's a cow, after all; you can put lipstick on it, but it's still a cow), but rather than raise the animal on a feed-lot for 14 short and brutish months, it's led to pasture, where it's allowed a full two years to reach maturity. And, because there has proven to be a market for grass-fed meats, it triples in wholesale value. Vegetables are raised organically and sold at farmers' markets where the producer and the consumer deal directly, increasing the profit margin for the former as the price decreases for the latter.

The value-added model explains why much of Hardwick's recent agricultural activity—indeed, why most local food efforts—revolves around high-end food. Organic tofu and soy milk. Blue cheese. Sourdough bread. Organic tomatoes ripened in biodiesel-heated greenhouses. If any of these farmers were trying to compete in the commodity market for soybeans, milk, wheat, or conventional tomatoes, they'd be crying into their coffee before they shipped the first crop. But by turning commodity into specialty, they can find a route to economic viability.

2. It must be based on sunshine.

For nearly 10,000 years, ever since agriculture began in the Fertile Crescent, a region that is now divided into Iraq, Syria, Jordan, Israel, and Egypt, sunshine has provided the energy to grow food through photosynthesis, the metabolic pathway that turns light energy into chemical energy. That chemical energy feeds the plant and the plant grows, eventually bearing or becoming whatever fruit or vegetable it was designed to bear or be. When soils became depleted, or where they lacked fertility, farmers (back then, "farmers" meant pretty much everyone) learned to enrich them through the practice of cover cropping, whereby a plant—usually a nitrogen-rich legume such as peas—is grown and then incorporated into the soil, where it rots into the earth and releases nutrients. In farming vernacular, cover crops are known as "green manure." Early agriculturists learned to include a green manure crop as part of the rotating crop schedule they used to keep disease and pests at bay.

If a farmer kept animals (most did, for milk, meat, and leather) such as sheep or goats or cows, he collected the manure and spread it on his cropland. In fact, in these early days of cultivation, every last scrap of fertility was utilized, including human manure. But whether it comes out of the hind end of an animal that walks on four legs or on two, brown manure is really just condensed, recycled sunlight, with a little stink thrown in to alert you that it ain't mud. The sun grows the grass, the animal grazes, digests, and does the inevitable number two, and the poop goes on the field to nourish the plants.

The agricultural revolution came and went without dramatically changing the art and science of fertility; most prominently, the Belgians discovered the nitrogen-fixing properties of clover and incorporated it into their rotations. Slowly, a degree of mechanization began to infiltrate the fields. But this early mechanization was of the pre-petroleum sort: seeders and plows and cultivators pulled behind the high, broad backs of oxen and horses. Farming was changing in scale, scope, and ambition, but it remained a practice that was nourished by the sun and practiced by almost everyone.

Things changed dramatically in the mid-1800s, when the German chemist Justis von Liebig realized that nitrogen could be applied to plants on its own, in the form of ammonia. Liebig's efforts at concocting a concentrated nitrogen fertilizer failed, both commercially and practically, but they were the first steps toward a chemical fertilizer industry that would quickly supplant sun-based fertility. In the late 1890s, average annual consumption of commercial fertilizers in the United States totaled 1,845,900 tons (it should be said that not all of this was chemical fertilizer; in these early days of the industry, much of the fertilizer was based on pulverized bone and bat guano); by the 1940s, that number had risen to 13,590,466 tons and by the '80s, it had hit 47,411,166 tons. At the same time, combustion engine technology gained traction, allowing fewer farmers to cultivate more acreage in what eventually became air-conditioned, GPS-navigated, MP3-playing comfort. The result was a dramatic drop in the number of person-hours required to grow 100 bushels of wheat—from 50 to 3. This was a monstrous achievement, and it has freed billions of people from trillions of hours of toil worldwide. Of the many technologies that have changed our lives over the past century, none has been as transformative as the agricultural innovations that have enabled us to pretty much ignore the sun.

But a tragic truth is becoming increasingly clear: It cannot continue forever. It's tragic because we've become utterly dependent on the chemicals and petroleum we use to outfarm the sun, and it's true because our agricultural system is now more vulnerable than ever. If ever the chemicals and petroleum stop flowing, we will go hungry; we simply can't have 1 person feeding 140 of us without these inputs. We probably can't have 10 people feeding 140. Maybe the demise of our petroleum-funded ag system will unfold slowly, as it seems to be now: death by a thousand paper cuts. Or maybe it will happen with a dramatic flourish: a bioterror attack, an oil embargo, or the sort of withering drought we've flirted with, but haven't really suffered with, since the Dust Bowl days. Or perhaps it will come on the back of an unintended consequence. The tremendous economy of scale delivered by our 21st-century system of farming has centralized food production like never before. Any kink in the system could generate a cascade of disruptions, idling the steady stream of trucks that barrel down our nation's interstates, pulling our dinners behind them.

A decentralized food system must, above all else, be resilient in the face of rapid, disruptive change. It must be capable of surviving a disruption in oil supply, fertilizer availability, and animal feed stocks. It should thrive in (or at least survive) periods of economic growth and contraction. It has to bend, not break, before the whims of nature and climate. To be clear, despite my disdain for the word "sustainable," I don't believe that the local food systems of today must run on sickle, scythe, and horse-drawn purity; instead, they need only be a step (or two, or three) in that direction. We have lost more than a century of knowledge, and in the process, massively inflated our agricultural expectations. We need to relearn those skills and reset our expectations, and any movement in this direction should be applauded. Chemical fertilizers and petroleum are to agriculture what easy credit was to the housing market, and we all know how that turned out. At some point, the air will come out of the agribusiness bubble, just as it came out of the housing bubble. At some point, petroleum and chemicals will be gone or, at the least, will have become so clearly untenable as to be unusable.

But the sun? That, hopefully, will still be there. Or else we've got even bigger things to worry about.

3. It must feed the locals.

It sounds absurdly obvious, doesn't it? Because really, what is the point of a local food system if the locals are still shuffling down supermarket aisles piling on the Cocoa Puffs and chicken fingers?

But perversely, this might be the toughest edict to fulfill, because it directly contradicts rule number one: *It must offer economic viability to small-scale food producers.* Once again, we run up against our own inflated expectations. Or, in this case, our *deflated* expectations. Because, for all its faults, the industrial agriculture system does one thing extraordinarily well: It fills our bellies for a fraction of what it cost our ancestors, or what it costs the citizens of other nations. The average European spends nearly 20 percent of his income on food, while his Bangladeshi counterpart spends 87 percent of her income to meet her daily nourishment needs.

Of course, it's become almost fashionable to discuss the hidden costs of our "cheap" food diet. They're real, and they matter, but the truth is that most Americans simply don't have the luxury of looking beyond the tangible metric of money in, money out. If you're bringing home $300 per week (as many in Hardwick do), you're not spending a heck of a lot of time thinking about the hidden toll of industrial agriculture. You're not considering its health costs, or the erosion of topsoil caused by monocropping, or even the backward logic of a subsidy system that pays farmers not to farm (or, conversely, to farm too much); you're too busy trying to find the Cocoa Puffs coupon tucked in your wallet.

Therefore, in order for a local food system to actually feed the locals, it must find a way around the cost issue. Calculating the carbon footprint of our diet is noble and all, but let's face it: To many working poor, who are struggling just to keep pace with the day-in, day-out fiscal demands of modern life, such exercises in eco-betterment are distractions for the well-off. Of course, the sad irony is that these are the people who stand to benefit most from vibrant, decentralized food systems.

Local food activists tend to argue that as energy and fertilizer prices rise, the price of commodity foods will rise, too. They say there will come a point when local foods—which are less reliant on these inputs—are actually cheaper than industrial foods. That may or may not happen; it seems equally plausible to me that inflated input prices might only compound the economy-of-scale advantage enjoyed by large-scale producers.

In any event, it seems foolhardy to wait for the price issue to resolve itself on the back of calamitous food inflation or for a disruption in our just-in-time supply chain to empty supermarket shelves in a matter of hours. The infrastructure and knowledge must be cultivated now, while we still enjoy relative plenty and stability. There's a Chinese proverb that goes something like this:

"What's the best time to plant a tree?"

"One hundred years ago."

"What's the second best time?"

"Today."

4. It must be circular.

Our current food system doesn't have much of a shape. It starts at one end, based on a river of nonrenewable inputs: nitrogen fertilizer is manufactured using natural gas, diesel fuel runs the farm tractors, the GMO seeds are engineered to tolerate farming practices that abuse the land. From there, it depends on more inputs to keep it chugging along on the straight line from field to processing plant to supermarket and, finally, to table. And there it finally ends, with whatever scraps remain being scraped into the garbage or fed to the dog. If the many failings of our industrialized food supply chain could be summed up in one image, it would look like a thin, straight line across a page.

The problem is that the page will eventually end; the line will run out of room. That's when we'll start to see skyrocketing food prices, shortages, and a growing awareness that something is not right in the world of agriculture. Any of that sound familiar?

The trick is to make our food system operate within the boundaries of that page; I describe it as a circular system, but in reality, it might be more oblong, with a few hard edges here and there, or an occasional triangular point. And, until we relearn everything we've forgotten and reset our expectations, it will probably veer off the page on occasion to benefit from a nonrenewable resource (most likely oil). But it always, always seeks to return, along the way seeking to benefit from fertility to be had from nearby: manure from the dairy farm down the road, food scraps from the local high school, or cover crops sown into fallow fields.

One of the great strengths of Hardwick's food system—indeed, one of the reasons I believe it has garnered so much attention—is the ease and clarity with which it articulates circular agriculture. Within a 10-mile radius of the town, you can find a seed producer, a composting operation, and numerous vegetable growers. These are not the only businesses participating in the region's farming circle, but they make it incredibly simple to demonstrate roundness in food production: The seeds are sown and grown into vegetables. The vegetables are served, and whatever scraps remain are turned into compost. The compost fertilizes the seed and vegetable crops. And so on. Heck, even if you've never given more thought to your food than deciding whether or not to ask for extra special sauce on your Big Mac, you can understand the relationship between compost, seed, and vegetable.

The circular food system has its limits, of course. If you live, as I do, in a northern clime, there will be no bananas in January. In fact, there will be no bananas ever, unless you stroll on down to Ecuador and pick a few bunches. If you live in the midst of a rural, Great Plains town, there will be no salmon or lobster. Processed foods will all but disappear; when that bag of Chips Ahoy in your pantry is gone, there won't be another, so enjoy it. No more Chips Ahoy, no more chicken fingers, no more McDonald's or Burger King. Food will almost surely be more expensive, at least in the most tangible respect: the price tag attached to it.

Clearly, this is a very different articulation of the food system than we've become accustomed to and clearly, it's not going to happen in a week, or a month, or even a year. It probably can't happen in a decade. The redrawing of our straight-line agriculture system into something even vaguely circular is a generational and perhaps multigenerational task. It's taken us more than a hundred years to get where we are; there's no reason to believe it will take us any less time to get back. Which means only one thing: We'd better plant our tree today.

———

To be honest, I'd assumed this list would be much longer. Perhaps it will grow. But I was also grateful that I could articulate my conceit in only four edicts; it seems a wholly manageable number. Sun-based. Economic viability. Local nourishment. Circular. When one considers the complexity of our modern industrial agriculture system, with its myriad inputs, subsidies, and global reach, my humble little list begins to seem almost . . . simple. Doable.

It surely won't be easy. Not for Hardwick, or for anywhere

else. The current agricultural landscape is such that some of these rules stand in direct opposition to others. How do you create economic viability for small-scale producers utilizing circular farming practices while still providing cost-competitive food that blue-collar Americans can actually afford? I don't know. How do you foster a wholesale shift in a society's expectations regarding what it eats and when? I don't know. How do you convince millions of Americans that a healthy, resilient food system depends on them becoming farmers, learning skills that have all but disappeared from our collective knowledge base? I don't know.

Maybe the reason Tom Stearns, Andrew Meyer, and all the other hardworking, well-meaning bodies and minds behind Hardwick's evolving food system haven't yet been able to answer my questions regarding the specifics of their grand experiment is the same reason I couldn't answer my questions. Maybe the madness and magic of the industrial food system we've created, its size and scope and seemingly indefatigable ability to churn out more and more food for less and less money, has severed any final, frayed connections that might have helped us grapple with these issues. Sixty years ago, nearly 40 percent of us lived on a farm. Now, it's less than 1 percent. Is it impossible to imagine an American landscape where 4 out of 10 of us produces food? Sadly, I think it is.

Of course, one could argue that we don't need 4 farmers for every 10 Americans, and that may be true. But there's no question that a decentralized agriculture system will require hundreds of thousands, if not millions, of us to pick up a shovel and start digging. And it will require the rest of us to accept very different versions of how we shop and what we eat. In the end, those may be the most difficult things of all.

CHAPTER SIX

I can't remember exactly when I became aware that something unusual was brewing in Hardwick, but it was probably about the time Andrew Meyer returned from his decade-long stint working on ag policy with the now-retired Vermont senator Jim Jeffords in Washington, DC. Jeffords, who'd made national news by leaving the Republican Party to become an independent in 2001, had always been a populist champion of Vermont's agricultural industry; in 2008, two years after his retirement, the University of Vermont broke ground on a 97,000-square-foot research and classroom facility for ag-based studies. It was named the James M. Jeffords Hall.

Meyer, who is in his late thirties, was reared on a hilltop dairy farm a few miles outside Hardwick, on a sweeping expanse of prime farmland, and has followed the well-trod path from farm to city and, as often happens, back to farm. He's also had the not-insignificant advantage of being born into a family of financial means; in this sense, his upbringing was vastly different from those of the majority of his fellow townspeople.

Meyer's return in 2004 made local news not for who he is, but for what he returned to do: open an organic tofu and soy milk processing plant in Hardwick, sourcing the beans from local farmers. At the time, there were no such facilities in Vermont; indeed, there were none within hundreds of miles. This isn't so surprising; after all, this is dairy country: calloused, blue-collar, truck-driving dairy country. Things like soy milk and tofu are viewed with suspicion and even outright disdain. I don't mean by everyone, of course: Vermont is a progressive state. There are vegetarians here and they are rarely the victims of open discrimination. Still, it can't be overstated just how audacious and unusual Meyer's scheme was. Tofu? Soy milk? In Hardwick?! He might as well have announced he'd be opening a Porsche dealership or a men's beauty salon.

Meyer's intentions were also notable for something else: He was the first to begin talking about the town using terminology like "movements" and "systems"; he was the first to spin the story of his hometown as one of redemption, not just for Hardwick, but for our beleaguered industrial, multinational food system. "We started whispering about Hardwick's food system in 2004 and 2005," Meyer told me. "Pretty much everybody laughed." Meyer is a forward-looking fellow; he knew they wouldn't be laughing for long.

Andrew Meyer knew a couple of other things, too: One, he knew that the broader American public is wrapping its increasingly flabby arms around the humble soybean, once deemed so unpalatable farmers wouldn't even feed it to their livestock. Man, oh man, how times have changed: Soy-food sales in the United States have exploded, from $300 million in 1992 to nearly $4 billion in 2004. And Meyer knew, as well as anyone could, how truly difficult it had become to earn a living the way Hardwick-area dairy farmers had traditionally earned a living: milking 30 to 60 cows and riding the roller coaster of wholesale milk prices.

The problem is this: Milk, like corn and wheat (and yes, soy), is a commodity product. It is priced by the hundredweight, which as you may have guessed, is 100 pounds. Of course, you and I don't buy milk by the pound, so it might be helpful to know that a gallon of milk weighs 8.6 pounds and (I'll save you the math) that there are 11.63 gallons in a hundredweight. A healthy, productive Holstein cow—Holsteins are the classic white-with-black-spots cattle that grace the postcards found in Vermont-themed gift shops—will give 50 to 70 pounds of milk per day, divided into two milkings. A cow's output depends on many factors, including where she is in her lactation (cows typically peak about two months after "freshening" with a calf and slowly drop off until they are "dried off," usually two months before they're due to freshen with another calf; ideally, they'll give birth to a calf each year), the quality of their feed (more protein begets more milk, to a point), their age (a cow will give milk well into her second decade, although most are culled after a few seasons of milking) and whether or not they're being injected with recombinant bovine growth hormone (rBGH), also known as recombinant bovine somatotropin (rBST). Cows secrete these hormones naturally; they're responsible for the production of insulin-like growth factor 1, which travels through the bloodstream to aid the breakdown of fats and help prevent mammary cell death. If you exist for the sole purpose of producing milk, mammary cell death is bad stuff, though it's a wholly natural part of bovine life.

According to Monsanto, the original producer of rGBH (Eli Lilly acquired the worldwide rights to the hormone in 2008), regular injections can increase milk production by 10 percent over the 300 days the average cow is milked annually. According to Australia, Canada, the European Union, Japan, and New Zealand, rGBH presents a human health hazard (to say nothing of the risk to cows) and milk from cows injected with the hormone cannot be sold in those countries.

The point of using the hormone in cows is to increase milk production for a given amount of feed input, which, issues of health aside, seems a worthy goal. In simple terms, the more milk that ends up in the bulk tank, the bigger the milk paycheck. But that's not the way it works. Farmers don't set the price for their milk. Instead, they take what the market is paying, and what the market is paying can change dramatically up or down over the course of months or sometimes even weeks. In May 2008, conventional milk was fetching $19.88 per hundredweight; by November, it had risen more than 30 percent, to $26.33. This sounds like a pretty good deal, until one considers the 80 percent increase in fuel and fertilizer costs and the

40 percent rise in feed prices from 2007 to 2008. And that, prior to these increases, the accepted break-even point for a hundredweight of milk was $20. And that, within six months of its November high, the price would plummet to less than half that—less than $12.

The long-term trends don't look so good either, because Americans aren't pouring nearly as many glasses of milk as they used to. Milk consumption in the United States peaked in 1945, at 46 gallons per capita, thanks in part to the World War II food-rationing program that excluded milk. But even discounting the rationing bump, the drop has been precipitous. In 1971, the year I was born, Americans were drinking 30.5 gallons of milk per capita. By 2005, that number had dropped to less than 21. Plotted on a graph, the decline looks as smooth and irreversible as a ski slope.

All of which is to say that Andrew Meyer saw an opportunity to exploit a runaway market while also providing an alternative to the remaining small family dairy farms scattered about the hills near his hometown. (The decline in milk consumption has been accompanied by an even more dramatic decline in the number of Vermont dairies, from 10,500 in 1954 to barely 1,000 today.) What if he could convince farmers to sow their fields with soybeans? Not all their fields, of course, but maybe a few back acres that had gone fallow. And what if, as the sole buyer of their beans, he could set the price, saving them from the whims of the commodity market? He could prove himself both a noble savior of the family farm and a shrewd businessman with a steely eye on the bottom line.

I first met Andrew Meyer in the front office of the Vermont Soy Company, a newly constructed, industrial-looking building clad in red corrugated-metal siding. The company had been launched the year before, in 2007, and the place still had the shine of something new. Andrew is of middling height and build; he wore a Vermont

Soy T-shirt tucked into a pair of blue jean shorts. His eyes are deeply set and he has one of those grins that make him look like he just got away with some sort of good-natured mischief. We pushed through a swinging door into the warehouse portion of his building, where 50-pound bags of soybeans were stacked high. He reached into a bag and extracted a handful, then extended his bean-filled palm. "See this?" he asked. "This is what you want: consistency. They're clean, the color's good, they're all the same." I nodded. They certainly did all look the same, a muted brown-green and about the size of a housefly. Meyer continued, "We want to be able to say 'You can taste the beans from Vermont.' And we want to keep that taste consistent."

The only problem was that, well, these beans weren't from Vermont. They were from Quebec, 100 miles and one country to the north. This, Meyer was keen to point out, represented an 11,900-mile reduction from the field-to-production-facility journey of the average soybean. "The ultimate goal is to have all our beans grown in Vermont. But the immediate goal is to have them grown as locally as possible, and right now, that's Quebec." Vermont Soy does source enough beans from Vermont that its firm tofu is made entirely of home-state soy. But Meyer admits that the curve has been steep: "Everybody's learning. How do you establish a contract and a price that works for everyone? How do you clean them? How do you store them? We can't make good milk out of bad beans." Which meant, for the time being, anyway, buying from Canadian producers.

We donned hairnets (a hairnet! I'd never worn a hairnet before) and pushed through another door, into the production room. The smell of soy was overpowering, cloying. It's a dank, wet smell, sharply at odds with the purported health benefits of the bean. Andrew's business partner, Todd Pinkham, stirred a vat of soy slurry. All around us were huge stainless-steel tubs and tanks and piping. The place had a sterile, futuristic aesthetic, despite the fact that much of the equipment was decades old, having been, rather ironically I thought, sourced from shuttered dairy farms.

Pinkham is Vermont Soy's secret weapon; tall and rail thin, he has devoted the majority of his adult life to soy. In 1996, a few years out of college, having dreams of farming but not the means to procure a farm, he started making tempeh, a fermented soy product that's usually sold in thin cakes, in his Morrisville, Vermont, home. "I couldn't afford a farm, so I started making tempeh" is how Pinkham put it to me, as if it were the most logical and natural leap in the world.

At first, it was five pounds a week, all of it produced in his kitchen sink, and all of it going to the Buffalo Mountain Food Co-op. This was the first incarnation of Vermont Soy, and it's a perfect example of how the co-op has long supported this sort of kitchen-sink business. Pinkham's tempeh operation grew steadily until he and his wife, Meg Treadwell, were supplying about 30 restaurants and food cooperatives around the state. By 2001, Pinkham and Treadwell were looking for factory space so they could expand their business. Then came September 11, 2001, and its accompanying recession, and everything ground to a halt. In hindsight, the setback served Pinkham well. He secured a grant from the USDA to develop soy-based products and used it to study manufacturing and marketing techniques for two years with Mingruo Guo, PhD, a Chinese-born professor of nutrition and food sciences at the University of Vermont in Burlington. And then Andrew Meyer came calling.

Vermont Soy is currently producing 10,000 pounds of tofu and 3,000 gallons of soy milk each month; the company sells most of its product in metro markets such as Boston and New York. Eventually, Vermont Soy hopes to double this output and to source the vast majority of its beans from the Hardwick region. To advance this cause, Meyer has offered workshops for farmers interested in cultivating soy, and he has done extensive field trials with High

Mowing Organic Seeds to determine which varieties deliver the best consistency and flavor.

I'd asked Meyer to show me a field of local soybeans destined for Vermont Soy, so one morning he met me in the barnyard of the 65-cow organic dairy run by his younger brothers, Nick and Taylor, who had agreed to cultivate four acres of a variety known as Ohgata. I arrived at 8:00, just as Nick and Taylor and their mother, Patty, were finishing the morning milking. Andrew was wearing rubber barn boots and a hooded pullover sweatshirt with the name of the family farm—North Hardwick Dairy—embroidered on the chest. For the first time, I noticed the streaks of gray in his hair. A 10-kilowatt wind turbine, installed just five months earlier, towered over us. The day was windless, so its blades were still, reflecting the bright morning sun.

The North Hardwick Dairy is the latest iteration of the farm on which Andrew and his three brothers were raised (the oldest brother, Tom, works in Washington, DC, as an economics consultant advising multinational companies). The family owns more than 400 acres on Bridgman Hill; for all of the Meyer boys' lives, the property has served as a working farm. "All through high school, we had farm chores. One of us would graduate, and the next would step up and take on more responsibility," Andrew said. I asked him if he'd ever resented the labor. "Not at all," he said. "Not even for a minute."

In 2003, Nick and Taylor decided to take over and expand the dairy operation from 35 to 65 cows. Andrew returned from Capitol Hill to help his brothers raise a pair of hoop barns with translucent roofs. They now stand on the landscape like huge, upside-down Us; the roof peaks rose to maybe 40 feet above my head, the height giving the space an airy, soaring effect. This is in stark contrast to the traditional Vermont dairy barns that dot the state's hills and hollows, which tend to be two-story affairs with a low-ceilinged milk room situated below a tall hayloft. The cows are fed and milked there, and they spend much of the winter in dark confinement.

Each of the 12 or so milk stations in the Meyers' milk room is equipped with a computer that reads microchips implanted in the cows. In this way, the brothers can monitor their broad-backed Holsteins for production, breeding dates, grain consumption, and so on, eliminating (or at least mitigating) the sort of eminently fallible guesswork and intuition most small-scale dairy producers rely on to husband their animals and, therefore, their livelihoods. Although I knew this sort of technology had long been commonplace at large dairy operations, I'd never seen it in person, and I couldn't help but feel somewhat unsettled by the digitization of the Meyers' cows. It's doubtful the chips are detrimental to the cows' health; in fact, it is likely that they allow the brothers to catch minor illnesses, or at least the indicators of illness—a drop in milk production, for instance—in their nascent stages. Yet the chips and computers represent a certain distancing of humans from the beasts on which they depend that feels to me unnatural and, in some indefinable way, less healthy.

Still, the North Hardwick Dairy is as light, airy, and pleasant an operation as any I've seen. The buildings are oriented to catch the morning light and designed for maximum airflow. Hell, I've *lived* in structures that aren't nearly as nice. The farm is certified organic, and for the previous four years, the Meyers had received the Highest Quality Dairy Award from the Vermont Dairy Industry Association. They ship their milk to the LaFarge, Wisconsin-based Organic Valley Family of Farms cooperative and sell a small amount of raw, unprocessed milk at the farm. Lately, the Meyers have been experimenting with growing sunflowers, hoping they can harvest the oil to run their farm machinery.

From a strictly visual perspective, I was drawn to the Meyers' operation in a way I hadn't expected or experienced on the many other dairy farms I've visited. It offered an aesthetic I'll call "orchestrated bucolic," which basically means that it was bucolic, but not for being bucolic's sake. There were functionality and purpose in it, and those qualities only added to the sensory pleasures of the place: the long views across hilltop pastures, the occasional soft murmur of a cow, the sweet smell of the fresh sawdust used for bedding. There were surely countless hours of labor and thousands of dollars invested in achieving this state, but at 8:30 in the morning on November 4, 2008, they simply weren't visible. Morning milking had just ended; Nick, Taylor, and Patty all seemed in high spirits. (This despite the fact that only a few hours before, Patty, who serves in the Hardwick Rescue Squad, had been called to the scene of a horrific car accident on Main Street. The car, piloted by a local youngster who'd had a wee bit too much to drink, had crashed into a building, caught fire, and torched the structure. The driver had walked away. It was, everybody seemed to agree, a very Hardwickian sort of incident.) They were probably thinking about breakfast and coffee, maybe a little downtime before returning to the barn to feed out the day's hay ration.

Andrew and I hopped into his truck and drove a half-mile up the road to where his brothers had planted the soybeans in early June. We stopped once so he could pick up a discarded paper plate on the roadway. A flock of 20 or so wild turkeys fled as we pulled up, running in a desperate, haphazard manner that suggested a lack of clearheadedness. They'd obviously been dining on the Meyer brothers' crop.

The soybeans were nearly ready to harvest. Andrew showed me how to press on a bean to gauge its readiness. "See how it's still a little gummy? Another couple days, and it should be perfect." The weather was stunning: already, at 9:00 a.m., it was almost 60°F and the sun was shining fiercely. This was a lucky break, and Andrew figured they might reap a half-ton of beans per acre, about half the fields' potential. Even such a modest harvest represented success: The year before, the Meyers had planted 12 acres of soy. The neighborhood deer population had eaten every last bean. "It looked like someone had come through with a lawn mower," said Andrew ruefully.

Northern Vermont is not naturally adapted to growing soy. It takes a full five months for the beans to mature, which means planting in early June (any earlier and the risk of a killing frost is too high) and hoping they don't get buried under an early snow. But I was learning that Andrew Meyer relishes the opportunity to succeed at something he's not supposed to succeed at. An hour earlier, standing under the windmill, he'd told me how he'd managed to help Jim Jeffords push through a landmark piece of legislation known as the Northeast Dairy Compact, which had put a floor under the price of commodity milk in the region. "I was the lead staff for the lead senator on the bill, which was a pretty amazing experience. It wasn't going very well. Even the lead sponsors declared it dead a couple of times. It wasn't supposed to pass, but we got it passed, anyway," Andrew said. A few minutes later, he'd pointed out the farm's quartet of dairy awards. "After we got the first one, everyone said, 'Oh, it's just a fluke.' Organic farms aren't supposed to get those awards. Now we've got three more and people are starting to think maybe there's something to the way we do things."

Andrew still helps out on the farm from time to time, milking when his brothers are out of town or putting up a cut of hay during the summer push. But most of his time is devoted to Vermont Soy and its sister business, Vermont Natural Coatings, which manufactures environmentally friendly, whey-based wood finishes. He envisions a day when all the beans for his company's tofu and soy milk are grown in the Hardwick region; he has calculated that it will take 75 to 100 acres of Hardwick soy to supply his company. I asked if his own mixed success at growing beans had dissuaded him at all. He shook his head. "When you say you're growing soybeans in Hardwick, it just says to people that anything's possible." This is probably true, though I knew I didn't need to remind Andrew that Vermont dairy farmers as a group are imbued with traditionalism and, in some cases, no small amount of obstinacy; just because something's possible doesn't mean they want to have anything to do with it.

We walked back toward Andrew's truck, soybean pods rubbing against our pant legs. Before opening the driver's door, Andrew turned back to the field. "This looks so much better than last year. We've learned a ton." He chuckled, laughing at just how much he didn't know. And perhaps how much he still has to learn.

Andrew Meyer is not the only member of Hardwick's agrepreneurial revolution trying to imagine an alternate future for Vermont's struggling family dairy farms. Shortly after I chased the turkeys out of the Meyers' soybean field, I found myself pulling into the barnyard at Jasper Hill Farm. It was 5:47 in the morning, which meant I was already 17 minutes late; Mateo Kehler, the dark-haired 39-year-old who owns the farm with his brother Andy, was waiting in the half-light of predawn. The lights in the barn behind him were on, and I could hear the shuffling of cows being milked.

The Kehler brothers operate two businesses on 223 acres of stony hillside just outside the town of Greensboro. The first is an artisanal-cheese-making outfit called Jasper Hill Farm, so-named not because it's located on an incline (which it is), but because the fellow who'd previously farmed it was named Jasper Hill. A second, closely related enterprise, located approximately a quarter-mile from where Mateo stood waiting for me at an hour that would normally find me drooling into my pillow, is called the Cellars at Jasper Hill. It consists of a 22,000-square-foot, $3 million, climate-controlled hole in the ground.

The brothers purchased the property in 1998, the same year Greensboro, population 770, lost five family-run dairy farms. They weren't exactly sure what they wanted to do with the place (early brainstorms included beer and baked tofu), but knew that they wanted to work the land in some manner and do something a little outside the box. This independent line of thinking was likely inherited from their parents, Thomas and Caroline, who moved to Bogotá, Colombia, in the mid-'60s on the Ford Foundation's third-world development program. Thomas Kehler launched two successful businesses in Bogotá; one was a hot dog company, and the second was Colombia's first cut-flower operation (the country now commands 11 percent of the $40 billion annual global cut-flower trade). With political violence reaching a fever pitch in the '70s, the Kehlers left Bogotá and moved to Vermont.

Soon after assuming ownership of Jasper Hill, having dismissed both beer and tofu as likely enterprises, Andy and Mateo turned their attention to cheese, in no small part because they viewed it as the most tangible way to model small-dairy viability. "We thought if we could demonstrate that you can make a decent living milking 50 cows, farmers would be lining up to see what we were doing," Mateo told me. We'd moved into the little kitchen that adjoins the cheese-making room and he was changing from his chore clothes into a pair of clean shorts and a long apron. Overhead, milk was pulsing through stainless-steel pipes on its way from the barn to the cheese room. Only minutes before, it had been in the udders of the Ayrshire cows that reside on the farm. By the time I left, at about noon, it would be cheese.

Although Jasper Hill soon garnered numerous accolades for its cheeses, which include a cloth-bound cheddar called Aspenhurst, a blue known as Bayley Hazen Blue, and a mold-ripened offering named Constant Bliss, that line of farmers they'd pictured did not instantly materialize. It turns out that milking 50 cows and ship-ping the milk to a bulk processor/distributor is a far cry from becoming a commercial farmstead cheese operation, which requires a significant infrastructure investment, specific knowl-edge, and a willingness to engage in marketing, selling, and dis-tributing one's product. Perhaps Jasper Hill can demonstrate the financial viability of the model. But it can't make anyone want to replicate it.

Hence that 22,000-square-foot, $3 million hole in the ground, with its seven arched concrete vaults extending from an atrium like fingers from a hand. It's convenient, of course, for the Kehlers to have such a facility at their disposal, but the cellars' true purpose is to serve as bait for other farmstead cheese makers. "The main intent is to lower the barrier of entry to new producers," Mateo told me, as he led me into the cellars, which have an annual capacity of 2 mil-lion pounds. On the day I visited, they were about 15 percent full with products from Jasper Hill and 10 other farmstead cheese mak-ers; to realize the cellars' full potential will require another 30 to 40 farms. It was cold (the cellars' climate is strictly controlled; temper-atures in individual aging rooms range from 39 to 55 degrees) and I shivered, but Mateo seemed unfazed. "They won't need to invest in the infrastructure and labor, and they don't have to build the mar-keting and sales components. These things don't replicate readily, and the average Farmer Brown just can't afford to take the risks."

Buying into the Kehler's vision isn't exactly risk-free: Even the relatively modest infrastructure necessary to make cheese can run a quarter-million bucks. But the rewards are at least commensurate with the upfront investment: It takes 10 pounds of milk to make 1 pound of artisanal cheese, which wholesales for between $3 and $11. The day I made cheese with Mateo, that same 10 pounds of milk was fetching a little more than a buck on the commodity market.

The Jasper Hill model might be unique to North America, but it's not exactly untested. Much of it is based on the example of Comté, a cheese produced exclusively in the Franche-Comté region of eastern France. Farmers there produce milk to strict specifications (for instance, only the milk of Montbéliarde cattle may be used, and each cow must be provided with at least a hectare of pasture) and deliver it immediately to village cheese makers who craft the cheese under the watchful eye and regulations of the *Appelation d'Origine Contrôlée*, the French agency charged with overseeing the country's many region-specific ag products. Comté is the most-consumed cheese in France. "It's totally socialist in a capitalist way," said Mateo, sounding almost dreamy. "Everyone in the chain is paid on quality, not production. It's a fundamentally different approach."

I didn't need to point out that such a fundamentally different approach might be challenging to implement among Vermont dairy farmers, because Mateo beat me to it. "The question is, will it translate culturally? How do you get a bunch of Yanks to band together?" He shrugged his broad shoulders, as if to say *Hey, I'm trying. Give me a break, here.*

What Andrew Meyer and Todd Pinkham are doing with Vermont Soy and what Mateo and Andy Kehler are doing with their businesses seem to me emblematic of the agricultural shift in Hardwick in many ways, and of the creative thinking necessary to wean ourselves from a food system run amuck. They're progressive, yet they seek to support traditional farming values. One of their primary goals is to create tangible economic gains for owners, employees, and suppliers. They endeavor to shrink the supply chain and market from their industry averages. Even the challenges are much the same: convincing obstinate old-timers to consider a new model.

Much the same could be said of Nick and Taylor Meyer and the North Hardwick Dairy. Everywhere I turned, there was evidence of the family's efforts to make the farm less dependent on resources that might soon be in short supply or crushingly expensive. There was the farm's organic designation, which meant there would be no chemical fertilizers applied to the fields and no growth hormone injected into the cows to promote milk production. It also meant the Meyers received nearly $30 per hundredweight for their milk. On the day I visited, this was nearly double the price of conventional milk; within a few months of my visit, it would be 300 percent more. There was the windmill, reducing the farm's reliance on electricity imported from distant generation sources. Sure, the sunflower crop had been disappointing—Nick had produced only 150 gallons of oil, enough to fuel the farm's big John Deere tractor for a week or maybe two of haying—but it was only the first year. Next summer would be better.

But there was something nagging at me, and after a time, I figured out what it was. The food that comes out of Vermont Soy's warehouse and the Cellars at Jasper Hill—and to a lesser extent the North Hardwick Dairy—seems out of place and time in the small town of Hardwick, Vermont. How many Hardwick residents actually eat soy products? A few, no doubt, but certainly not the majority. And how many of them can afford to buy cheese that costs upwards of $20 per pound? At least in part, the lack of a local market is why these businesses court markets in Boston, New York City, and even San Francisco. And the organic milk being pumped out of Nick and Taylor's bulk tank would end up retailing for more than $5 per gallon. I know how much work goes into a gallon of milk, and $5 is marginal recompense. But let's not forget, this is a pickup-driving town with a tractor-repair shop, a gun store, and a lumberyard making up a sizeable percentage of the business landscape. These people are not lining up for organic milk lattes and tofu smoothies. If the founders of Vermont Soy, Jasper Hill, and the North Hardwick Dairy are truly committed to building a local food economy, shouldn't they commit themselves to producing foods the locals can afford to eat? And actually will? Because, when you bore right down into it, past the economics and the politics and everything else, isn't that the heart of the whole matter?

I was beginning to understand that the issue of affordability would color almost every aspect of this story, and I was reminded that a truly successful decentralized food system would be the one that bridges the financial divide and puts local food into the mouths of local people while leaving enough of their $300 paychecks intact so they can meet the needs of shelter, transportation, and health care. And I was reminded that, frankly, no one I'd talked to seemed to have any idea how to make this happen. The Meyer and Kehler families have built businesses that are based on localized food production, but not on feeding the locals, a distinction that forced me to think hard about what a local food system really, truly needs to contribute to its community. If such a system must feed the locals (as I've so presumptuously declared) and these businesses, by and large, don't, does that make their efforts a failure? Or is it enough to use locally produced food as the vector for fair-wage jobs, leaving the decisions about what to do with that money—blow it on cheese puffs, pay the mortgage, buy a plasma TV—up to their employees? Because we're talking about a food *system*, maybe it's unreasonable to expect every single business within that system to fulfill every single edict. Maybe we should measure the system as a whole, rather than turning a critical eye toward each individual enterprise. I recalled something Mateo Kehler had said as we stood waiting for flocculation, the precise moment in the cheese-making process when the milk begins to gel: "As far as I'm concerned, all this is really about creating opportunity." He was talking about what he does, but also about the whole Hardwick agrepreneurial revolution. "Sure, we could probably feed ourselves, but is that a reasonable, realistic goal? Vermont has always been a net exporter of ag products. I don't think that's about to change, so why not at least try to create some vibrancy in agriculture?" He looked up at me, and grinned. "But then, what the hell do I know?"

Vermont Soy, the North Hardwick Dairy, and Jasper Hill are examples of small-scale, decentralized food production as economic driver. To a certain extent, this is true of each of Hardwick's food producers; they all exchange their wares for US currency and most distribute a good bit of this currency throughout the region in the forms of wages and spending. And it's not as if no one in the community is consuming the goods being produced by these businesses. You can walk into the Buffalo Mountain Food Co-op and purchase tofu made less than a mile down the road and cheese produced a modest bicycle ride away at Jasper Hill; Nick and Taylor sell a small quantity of milk directly to friends and neighbors. But the overwhelming majority of each business's product is shipped far beyond Hardwick's town line and traded for dollars that may or may not stay in town, that may or may not be used to support the local economy or be directed into the pockets of the same multinational, food-by-corporation interests that have brought us to such a powerless place.

This is not so much a criticism of these specific businesses as a commentary on the broader system that offers few choices to consumers wanting to effect some level of reform. Clearly, Hardwick needs good jobs at least as much as other communities, and the jobs at Vermont Soy and Jasper Hill pay better than many and provide safe, pleasant working conditions (and, if you're one of the 17 employees at Jasper Hill, you'll get two cords of firewood and a butchered hog as an annual bonus). They may even offer a level of security that we can no longer take for granted: In January 2009, when the national news seemed little more than a depressing litany of job losses, Vermont Soy was hiring. Nick and Taylor don't employ much outside help, but their operation requires a fair amount of servicing by local businesses in the form of equipment repair, grain sales, building materials, and the like.

If there's an irony in marketing an ag business as part of a local food economy and then shipping its product outside the region, it's not lost on me. But it's also not lost on me that the term "local food economy" includes the "e" word and that we are all, for better or worse, part of the larger economy that keeps us all clothed, sheltered, and fed.

CHAPTER SEVEN

Barely a mile down the road from the North Hardwick Dairy, just as Bridgman Hill Road crests and flattens to run along a high ridge of open fields, there's another dairy farm. It sits on the opposite side of the road; this could be seen as metaphoric, but that's probably reading too much into it. I'd passed the farm on my way to the Meyers' operation, and even then I'd thought that it fit my long-standing notion of what a small, family-run Vermont dairy should look like. This is not to say that it was particularly picturesque: Innumerable pieces of machinery in varying states of disrepair lay scattered about like the carcasses of large animals, and while the long, wood-sided barn appears structurally sound, it would benefit from a coat of paint—ideally about 20 years ago. The farmhouse, immediately to the right of the barn, shares this weathered and time-worn aesthetic.

This is the farm of Forrest Foster and Karen Shaw. It is home to perhaps 60 cows, maybe half of which are being milked at any one time, and about 70 pigs in stages of growth ranging from newborn (one of the sows had pigged only two days prior to my initial visit) to mature breeding stock. A recently constructed equipment shed houses a massive log skidder and various piles of farm-related detritus. The Foster Farm is certified organic; it ships its milk to the Organic Valley cooperative, the same one that purchases the Meyers' milk.

I'd come to Forrest and Karen because they are, in the parlance of the region and their craft, old-timers. This doesn't so much mean that they're old (age is only one of the components of old-timerism) as it means that they possess skills and values that once defined rural American life and are now largely forgotten. They milk cows, raise hogs, keep extensive gardens, make maple syrup, log, and put up a tremendous quantity of food, much of which they sell, barter, or simply give away to those in need.

When I arrived, Forrest was at a neighboring farm owned by a young couple named Heather and Chad Trudeau. They'd bought the farm and moved from Connecticut exactly a year prior, when conventional milk was fetching more than $20 per hundredweight. The most recent check the Trudeaus received had paid just over $15 per hundredweight, and state officials were predicting $10 milk within months. The Trudeaus keep a herd of 99 mostly Holstein cows, a scale that means they either work 100-hour weeks or hire help; the looming specter of $10 milk made the choice for them, and Forrest had volunteered his services, at least until the snow melted and the demands of a farm in spring forced his full attention to his own operation.

I found Forrest in the Trudeau's milk room, swabbing the teats of the huge Holsteins with an iodine-and-lanolin concoction that disinfects and moisturizes, sort of like Palmolive for the bovine set. I realize this may sound unflattering, but I mean it in the most endearing way possible: Forrest Foster looks exactly like Elmer Fudd, or at least what I would expect a 60-year-old, flesh-and-blood version of Elmer Fudd to look like. He wore a plaid-patterned wool hunting cap with turned-up sides, and there was an appealing roundness to his face that was accentuated by his mouth, which seemed to be in a constant state of grinning. There's an immediate sense of good-natured mischief about Forrest that makes me want to be in his company. "I'm just playin' with tits," is how he greeted me (which of course is exactly what he was doing), and when I asked him where he went to high school, he grinned hugely and said, "Out behind the barn," before explaining that he had actually started school, but had dropped out in large part because he was "flirting with the girls pretty good and couldn't concentrate." He wore a button-down shirt that was splattered with cow shit and tucked into a pair of similarly adorned work pants. On his belt, he'd hung a skrench, the half-screwdriver, half-wrench tool used to adjust the tension of chain-saw chains. In a room adjacent to the milking station, a pair of enormous winter squashes, a jar of homemade ketchup, and two jars of homemade jam sat on a table. Forrest had brought them from his and Karen's pantry for Heather and Chad.

It was just after 5:00 p.m. when I arrived at the Trudeaus; the evening milking was about half over, and I hung out with Forrest and Heather as they milked the cows in batches of eight. There was a relaxed rhythm to it; Heather, a thin, pretty woman sporting a pair of well-manicured eyebrows and a pink sweatshirt (or mostly pink; it, too, was streaked with wet brown), would usher the cows into the milking station, which was constructed on a platform, so that the bulbous, milk-swollen udders hung at chest level. Forrest then sprayed each teat, followed by a wipe down from Heather, and then they both attached the vacuum-pump milking machines. Each round of cows was in and out the door in less than a quarter-hour.

As we talked, mostly about the dire state of the economy (Forrest: "It's kind of a stressful time in every situation. It's a good time to help out a neighbor") and the strange, often-illogical lure of farming (Heather: "The other day I went out into a whiteout to feed the calves and I thought 'What the hell am I doing?' And then I thought, 'I wouldn't change a thing'"), it occurred to me that there was a good chance that Heather and Chad Trudeau would not survive the collapse in milk prices. Perhaps they had family money or an ample line of credit; perhaps they simply had the will and ability to work harder and more efficiently than most. Maybe they would be among those that endured the coming shakeout. But there was no question that everything about their model—the conventional, family-size dairy—placed them squarely in the cross-hairs of the looming collapse in milk prices.

After the last Trudeau cow was milked, Forrest and I walked out into the dark. It was a beautiful night; it had been a cold winter thus far, but on this evening temperatures were in the 20s, and a wisp of clouds couldn't obscure the stars. It was 6:30 and there were still Forrest's cows to milk, but he paused before climbing into his big Ford pickup. He'd clearly been thinking about the same things I had. "I've been here over 30 years and this is the first time I've had neighbors that I really liked." He sighed. "I don't see how they're going to make it."

The irony, of course, is that much the same could have been said about Forrest Foster at almost any point in his farming career, which has spanned pretty much his entire life. He was raised on a small farm in nearby Walden, where he milked 13 cows with his father, Francis, by hand. The Foster family, with its 13 children and modest, labor-heavy, self-reliant lifestyle, was representative of the time and place. At some point when Forrest was in his twenties, he and his father had had a falling out (the exact circumstances weren't entirely clear to me, but it seemed to have something to do with his father's purchase of a sawmill and his attention to the farm, which Forrest prized, subsequently waning) and Forrest ended up on the 135-acre farm owned by Karen Shaw, whose first husband had left the year before because, according to Karen, "he realized farm animals smell." Forrest does not often leave the Hardwick region; he has never been on an airplane, and he's been to Burlington, Vermont's largest town, only once (it's an hour away), to appear in court when he and Karen sued the Agri-Mark dairy cooperative over management issues. He worn barn boots covered in manure into the courthouse, and Forrest and Karen won the case.

He and Karen have always sold food directly off the farm. For a time, they would leave bottles of raw, unpasteurized milk in the cooler at the Buffalo Mountain Food Co-op for convenient pickup. "It wasn't legal, so I wanted to be in on it," he told me through his omnipresent grin. That practice has since been discontinued, but the Fosters still sell milk directly off the farm, which is entirely legal and therefore probably not nearly as satisfying to Forrest. Every year, he slaughters dozens of hogs, cuts and wraps them, and distributes them as he sees fit, on a sliding scale that might range from $3 per pound to, well, nothing. "I've always wanted to get food direct to people. Sometimes, the people don't have any money." Forrest said this matter-of-factly, as if he were commenting that some people don't have blue eyes, but what the hell, he'd be sure they got fed, too. We were standing in his milk room as he assembled the modest apparatus he uses to empty his cows' udders. In the Foster/Shaw barn, there are no computers, no chest-high, eight-cow milking platform. There are only Forrest and Karen, stooping next to each of their tawny Jerseys to apply the small pumps, which empty into buckets whose contents are transferred to another, larger vessel, which is finally upended into the bulk milk tank at the front of the barn.

I followed Forrest into the depths of his barn, where his cows stood in individual stanchions. One of Forrest's five children, Forrest Jr., who is in his mid-twenties, was plunging a chain saw into a large, round bale of hay in order to loosen its frozen center. A couple of nights earlier, Forrest Jr., had suffered a seizure while driving his father's big one-ton pickup and nosedived into a telephone pole. The truck was nearly totaled; Forrest Jr. seemed none the worse for wear. Forrest seemed nonplussed, though he allowed it was rather inconvenient to be without the truck for a time.

The chain saw roared, but Forrest paid scant attention to the cacophony; he just kept grinning and talking, as if the earsplitting noise were nothing more than a distant mosquito. Since I couldn't hear a damn thing he was saying, I let my eyes wander around the barn, which belonged in the same category as the Meyers' grand and soaring structure in name and purpose only. The Foster/Shaw barn, as I've noted, almost perfectly fit my vague notion of what a small, family-farm barn should look like: The ceiling of the milk room was low and laced with spiderwebs and long strings of dust, and everything seemed to tilt in one direction or another. The whole effect made me feel slightly vulnerable, and I had to remind myself that the barn had probably been standing for 100 years or more, so it would likely make it through this night, too. In one sense, the Foster/Shaw barn is deficient when measured against the modern facility up the road. It is darker and dirtier and in many ways feels like a relic from another era. But in another sense, the one that accounts for the emotional and perhaps spiritual appeal of a working farm, this barn felt the richer. The lack of mechanization—Forrest and Karen's little milk-can vacuum system is only one step removed from hand milking—brings with it a level of human-to-animal contact that's simply absent at modern facilities like the Meyers' and, to a lesser extent, the Trudeaus'. Every time Forrest milked a cow, he knelt at her flanks, absentmindedly stroked her side, and attached the four vacuum receptacles to her teats. Sometimes he remained on one knee next to his cow while the pump pulsed and sucked; sometimes he stood to scrape a fresh pile of poop into the gutter or to talk to me, or to prep the next cow for milking. But by any measure, no matter the precise order and timing of his routine, he engaged with his animals on a level that's become unusual on most farms. Can the intuition that results from decades of this engagement—the stooping, the stroking, the constant contact—outperform the computerized monitoring systems that have become the norm? I don't know, and no doubt there's a reason the industry has evolved into the digital age, but there's no question in my mind which one *feels* better.

Admittedly, this is based on my somewhat romantic, decidedly human view of things. If I were a cow, would I prefer the dim confines of Forrest and Karen's barn or the airy, light-filled shelter up the road at the Meyers'?

We'd been in the barn for about 30 minutes and Forrest had milked only four cows. He seemed in no hurry, despite the fact that his current pace would mean he'd finish milking around 11:00, only six hours before he'd have to rise and do it all over again. It was at about this time that Karen walked into the barn, cast a sideways, suspicious glance my way, and without a word started scooping poop. I retracted the hand I'd offered for shaking and went back to recording Forrest's nearly endless stream of commentary in my notebook. This got Karen's attention: "What're you taking notes for?" she asked sharply, turning the full intensity of her steely eyes my way. Oh boy.

Karen thawed a bit as I explained myself, and we started discussing the particulars of Hardwick's agrepeneurial movement. Which is not, for a moment, to suggest that she approves of it, a stance shared by her husband. In Forrest's and Karen's views, the agrepreneurial movement only threatens the low-key, neighbor-to-neighbor food system that has long defined their lives as farmers and Hardwick residents. "That's what it boils right down to," Forrest told me from the side of a particularly sway-backed Jersey. "We live that way and they're glamorizing it. And they've got all the money. This is going to ruin the small, local farms. Pretty soon you're not going to need little farms like mine. They're going to run us off." Karen nodded in agreement. Forrest lapsed into a rare moment of contemplative silence, then quickly brightened. "I got some of Andrew's soy milk from the food pantry. I guess they couldn't get rid of it. My pigs like it pretty good."

I thought this was pretty funny, but in at least one sense, it's indicative of a functioning food system, whereby the waste of one producer becomes the resource of another, and it wouldn't be the only time Forrest and Karen benefited from the agricultural infrastructure being developed around them: A few days later, a flatbed trailer arrived in their barnyard with 8,000 pounds of water buffalo cheese from the Cellars at Jasper Hill. The cheese had gone off, testing too high for a bacterium that could sicken humans but would be harmless to pigs. Forrest had wrapped a huge chain around the whole hulking pile and pulled it off the truck with his log skidder; for the remainder of the winter, his hogs would fatten on artisanal cheese that normally retails for more than $15 per pound.

I left the Foster/Shaw barn at about 9:00, stepping into temperatures that had dropped considerably from what had greeted Forrest and me outside the Trudeau barn. The snow-covered ground reflected the moonlight with an eerie glow. Behind me, I knew, Forrest was kneeling beside another cow and Karen was scraping shit into the gutter. In a couple of hours, they too would emerge from the barn and enter their home. The house was built before the era of insulation; it would be cold, and they would stoke the fire.

As I pulled out of the barnyard, I couldn't help but think that everything about the Foster/Shaw farm was from an earlier era of agriculture. And I couldn't help but hope that it portends something of its future.

CHAPTER EIGHT

Clearly, there was some tension developing in town. I must admit, I hadn't seen it coming, but this lack of foresight is more a reflection of my own naivete than a comment on the probability of said tension developing, which, I have come to understand, was approximately 110 percent.

Consider a small, close-knit rural town, inhabited in large part by folks who'd chosen the town as much for what it wasn't as for what it was. Not so long ago, there was nothing hip or pretentious about Hardwick. Not so long ago, for better or worse, no one much cared what happened in Hardwick, except for those who called it home. Not so long ago, Hardwick was just a small town with a few good stories in its past and a few mildly amusing jokes circulating at its expense. What might happen when suddenly that town becomes the subject of a feature story in the *New York Times* and numerous articles elsewhere and when the people featured in those stories belong to a fresh-faced generation of agriculturists who aren't afraid to talk as if they have the answers to some mighty big questions?

And what if the authors of those stories didn't take the time (or, perhaps even worse, didn't even *know* they should take the time) to consider the quieter, long-standing agricultural efforts in town? I cannot speak for anyone else, but I believe that my failure to acknowledge these efforts in my *Gourmet* article was, in a strange way, indicative of the success of these businesses. I've lived in the broader Hardwick region for most of my adult life and shopped at the Buffalo Mountain Food Co-op for more than a decade. I've bought lettuce from Surfing Veggie Farm, broccoli from Riverside Farm, strawberries from Hazendale Farm, bread from Patchwork

Bakery, and so on. These humble agricultural enterprises have nourished me for years, and before I started writing this book, I'd rarely if ever considered them. They've become so ingrained in the community that I've taken them for granted. Think about that for a moment: What do we take for granted? That which has proven utterly dependable and satisfactory. That which is so wildly successful, we never question it.

Not long after I started writing this book, I received a long e-mail from my friend Steve Gorelick, who lives on a 40-acre homestead in Walden, just outside Hardwick. Steve and his wife, Suzanna Jones, milk a couple of goats and one cow and sell blueberries at the Hardwick farmers' market and the Buffalo Mountain Food Co-op. They also sell milk and goat cheese to neighbors. They are close friends with Forrest Foster and Karen Shaw. Over the 10 years I've known them, I've come to regard them as passionate and articulate critics of corporate culture, and I've come to respect them for their unflinching resolve to live a low-impact life. Their home is powered exclusively by solar photovoltaic panels and they heat their water with solar collectors. In fact, they don't even own a gas or electric hot-water heater, an appliance that is utterly ubiquitous in the modern American home.

Like Forrest and Karen, Steve and Suzanna are not particularly impressed with the latest iteration of Hardwick's agricultural infrastructure. Steve's e-mail read, in part:

> What I see is a group of entrepreneurs capitalizing on the wave of interest in local food. Nothing wrong with that, more power to them, but please don't give them credit for creating that wave or pushing it substantially forward. You'll notice they didn't have the temerity to call their organization the Center for a Local Food Economy. Their emphasis on value-added products is implicitly related to

exporting food out of the local region, with the Vermont name as part of the value that's been added. Doing that means undermining local food production elsewhere—the same old model of shipping food to where it gets the highest price. Can't blame them: You can't get rich selling local food to local people, and I think these guys are largely motivated by the desire to make a lot of money.

Could this be true? Actually, I knew some of it was: the emphasis on added value, for instance. There was no denying that. Soybeans are sold on the commodity market; tofu is not. Milk is sold on the commodity market; blue cheese is not.

And the push into markets far beyond Vermont's boundary line? That was true. High Mowing sells its seeds all over the country. Vermont Soy is prying its way into Boston and New York City outlets. Jasper Hill ships cheese to San Francisco. I'd heard discussion of creating a Hardwick "brand," of how cool it would be if Whole Foods devoted an entire display to Hardwick, if the town could somehow create a proprietary *brand* and use that *brand* to leverage sales and profits.

Which led me to the money. That was true, too, and I knew it was so because on numerous occasions, Tom Stearns had articulated his desire to become wealthy so that he might launch more businesses. He called himself a "serial entrepreneur." Meyer's Vermont Soy needed money, too: They had built a processing plant, set up a distribution network, and were pressing hard to expand the company. And the boys at Jasper Hill could hardly afford to settle into stasis. They were sitting on 22,000 square feet of cheese cave and in hock for seven figures. Their monthly loan repayment was north of $20,000. That's not the sort of scratch you raise by selling solely to a town of 3,200 blue-collar residents.

Looking back over Steve's e-mail, I realized that, viewed from a

certain angle, the whole damn thing was true. And I believed there
was another problem that he hadn't even mentioned: Sure, on one
level, these new agricultural entrepreneurs were providing for the
locals. They'd generated numerous jobs and placed their products in
local outlets, including the Buffalo Mountain Food Co-op. But there
was a tangible sense that there'd been a lot of self-aggrandizing talk,
that a feedback loop was developing between these companies and
the media, and that perhaps it was time for them to shut up and get
down to business. It didn't help that two of the businesses being featured most prominently sold cheeses that cost $20 per pound and
soy milk that ran $4 per quart. As usually happens, the local paper
was the first to tap into the backlash. After running a series of articles on the recent developments in the town's ag sector, the *Hardwick
Gazette* ran a front-page story on the national media's failure to
acknowledge the region's long-standing agricultural efforts.

The *Gazette* story made me wonder how much of the fuss was
provoked by the media's fawning. Indeed, the *New York Times* article seemed to be an instigating factor. I hadn't heard any dissent
prior to the Gray Lady's attentions, even as I worked on my *Gourmet* article. That doesn't mean it wasn't there; it's easy to imagine
how seeing the story splashed across the *Times*'s page might serve
as a flash point, igniting tensions that had long been smoldering. If
the media had never sunk its claws into Hardwick and the agrepreneurs had simply kept doing what they do, would Forrest, Karen,
Steve, and Suzanna have been so disturbed by it all? Steve's e-mail
even hinted that the issue might not be so much what the agrepreneurs were doing, but how the media had chosen to portray what
they were doing: "What I see is a group of entrepreneurs capitaliz-
ing on the wave of interest in local food. Nothing wrong with that,
more power to them, but please don't give them credit for creating
that wave or pushing it substantially forward."

But the agrepreneurs and the media were not operating in

separate vacuums. In this regard, perhaps the media could even be credited for explaining to the people of Hardwick just what the hell these folks were up to. Because there had been, as far as I could tell, little in the way of direct communication between the agrepreneurs and the other citizens of the region. Everything was being filtered through the media lens, and all the material that was being filtered had been provided by the agrepreneurs themselves. This meant at least two things: One, that these efforts were being cast in the most positive, inspiring light possible, and two, that the filter itself would further distill this information into whatever angle a particular outlet had decided fit its needs best. Which means, basically, whatever story would sell.

So the story that was being told over and over wasn't necessarily wrong or demonstrably false. But it was, unambiguously, determined by the agrepreneurs and the media outlets themselves. It's not hard to understand how such treatment could rub folks the wrong way. Perhaps they simply felt left out; perhaps they didn't like being told what was happening in their community by a newspaper headquartered in New York City. And it's not hard to imagine that such treatment could lead to a rather shallow elucidation of the broader story. To me, it sometimes seemed as if there were a lot of grand ideas, good intentions, and inspiring sound bites, but the tangibles had yet to evolve. I recall trying to pin down Stearns on his claims of creating a local food system that could be blueprinted and exported to other communities. But what I should have asked him (and what I vowed I would) was this: What *won't* you be exporting? Because it was the stuff that would stay in Hardwick—the food, the jobs, the resilience—that really mattered. Simply put, if Hardwick's needs weren't met, the blueprint was faulty.

And what the hell was the deal with the Center for an Agricultural Economy? "A wannabe locavore circle jerk," was how one particularly cynical friend described it. I thought this was pretty mean (but okay, yes, sort of funny), but it probably reflected the fact that no one could really figure out why it existed. Its Web site says, "The mission of the Center for an Agricultural Economy . . . is to engage agricultural leaders in the emerging 21st century food system to build capacity and inspire the public in supporting and implementing this system." Well, now, that doesn't exactly clear things up, does it? Every so often, I'd stroll past the center's freshly minted office on Main Street and peer through the windows. Often, it was empty, but sometimes I'd see Monty Fischer, the executive director, jawing on the phone. Now, whoever was on the other end of that call was most likely critical to the success of Hardwick's agricultural economy, and whatever they were talking about was surely pertinent. But I could see how, in a dirt-under-the-fingernails town like Hardwick, a middle-aged fellow dressed in a button-down shirt talking into a telephone in a newly renovated office could be seen as somehow superfluous to the region's farm economy.

Yes, I could understand *how* some of the criticism had formed; the underpinnings of tension and criticism were not terribly difficult to identify. But to what extent was this criticism constructive or even valid? Sure, it was part of Hardwick's evolving food-system narrative. But was it truly substantive? Did it offer a viable alternative? I was honest with Steve and Suzanna; I told them I wasn't entirely swayed by their line of reasoning, that I wasn't prepared to abandon the agrepreneurial movement simply because it sought to profit from the sale of food and much of that profit was being lifted from pockets in distant cities.

So they set out to change my mind. In the middle of February, they invited me to dinner. They were unambiguously honest regarding their objective: This was not to be a social visit; this was not about light conversation or even vigorous debate. This was to be a brainwashing. That's not entirely fair, of course, but there was no doubt that they hoped to shift the focus I had on Hardwick's agrepreneurial revolution and, quite possibly, free market capitalism itself. Frankly, I was a bit wary, for Steve Gorelick and Suzanna Jones are as passionate as they come. I suffered a brief paranoid fantasy that they were setting me up, that I'd find myself bound and gagged in their basement, fed sour goat's milk, forced to read repeatedly from the works of Wendell Berry and anarcho-primitivist (look it up) Derrick Jensen. But then, they *were* offering up a pan of homemade lasagna and a blueberry pie. I deemed the risk acceptable and took the bait.

The Gorelick-Jones household is located at the edge of a small, sloping field in the town of Walden. There is no utility service to any of the handful of homes along their road; a few years ago, when a parcel of land across the road came up for sale, Steve and Suzanna bought it, assuring themselves the right to deny access to the power company and, coincidentally, to slow the spread of development by ensuring that anyone who chooses to build along that stretch of road will have to live without access to grid electricity. Their house is charmingly rustic and weather-worn. There are two barns on the property. Both are small, sided with unpainted boards and on the backside of their life spans. One is home to a half-dozen goats, the other provides safe haven to a milk cow and her calf. Steve and Suzanna keep chickens, tend extensive gardens, and husband a prolific blueberry patch. Like Forrest Foster and Karen Shaw (of whom they speak with reverence), they sell, barter, and flat-out give away the food they produce according to an undefined metric of need.

I'd known Steve and Suzanna for nearly a decade; they were among the first people my wife and I met when we moved to Cabot, in part because they have children (Ezra and Talia) close in age to our own and in part because our lifestyles are remarkably similar. We both keep small farms, we both run our homes on solar power, and we both have chosen frugal lifestyles intended to minimize consumption and dependence on off-farm jobs. To be sure, they have done this better and more thoroughly than us, perhaps because, at 58 and 47, they have, collectively, 27 years more practice. Suzanna homeschools Ezra and Talia, farms, and, if my experience of her is any indicator, spends a lot of time on the phone bemoaning the changes in Hardwick. Steve works three-quarter time for a non-profit called the International Society for Ecology and Culture (ISEC), which, according to its mission statement, exists for the purpose of "promoting locally based alternatives to the global consumer culture." He is also coauthor of a book called *Bringing the Food Economy Home* and is producing a documentary film titled *The Economics of Happiness*. I couldn't help but notice that ISEC's mission doesn't sound so different from the mission statement of the Center for an Agricultural Economy, the Hardwick ag organization that so arouses Steve's and Suzanna's ire.

I arrived at their home just as the last tendrils of daylight were fading; the house was dimly lit in a way folks who live off-grid are unanimously familiar with. When the full extent of your home's electricity is what can be captured by the sun and stored in a bank of batteries, efficiency often trumps seeing with optimum clarity. Talia was plinking out "Twinkle, Twinkle Little Star" on an old upright piano, Ezra was drawing at the dining room table, and Suzanna was scurrying about the kitchen, where a wood-burning cookstove was giving off a nice blanket of warmth. Steve was in the basement loading the woodstove that heats the house. (There are a total of three woodstoves in the house, and exactly zero heaters that utilize fossil fuels.) It was a cozy, wholesome scene, and I tried to see it as someone from, say, the suburbs of New Jersey would see it, but of course, I couldn't. As atypical and *Little-House-on-the-Prairie*-ish as the Gorelick-Jones household might seem to suburban America, it's simply not that unusual in the hills of rural northern Vermont.

Suzanna dished up enormous plates of lasagna, and we sat around the table under the half-light of a compact-florescent bulb.

Suzanna spoke first, leaning forward in her chair, her lean face framed by long hair going gray: "What's the difference between a character and an entrepreneur?" I might have responded, but she wasn't inclined to give me the chance, having already launched into the answer before I could open my mouth. "A character grows from the land. An entrepreneur grows from economies." She was quoting the late Vine Deloria Jr., an American Indian author, historian, theologian, and activist. Deloria, along with Derrick Jensen, Wendell Berry, and food-sovereignty activist and environmental thinker Vandana Shiva are all featured prominently on Suzanna Jones's bookshelves and have obviously helped shape her worldview.

In any case, I understood what she was saying and, to a certain extent, I could see it in the people of Hardwick. It did seem as if the region's true agricultural *characters*, the ones so full of personality and quirk and some indefinable quality that evoked (in me, anyway) respect and resolve, were products of the land on which they lived and worked. I thought of Forrest Foster and Karen Shaw.

Suzanna went on: "There are two currencies in our world: There's the currency of money and the currency of nature. The currency of money is the one that's failing us now." My mouth was full of lasagna again—damn, it was good—so I just nodded. I got that, I really did, and I'm willing to bet that an increasing number of my fellow Americans are beginning to get it, too. "If you agree with that, if you understand that this whole system is a failure . . ." She trailed off, then made the connection: "Tom Stearns's approach to agriculture has so many elements of that system that it's not an alternative. It's all based on the currency of money. What do people really need? They don't need convenience; they need food, clothing, shelter. They don't need this gentrified green, boutique scene." One of the things I've learned about Suzanna Jones is that the more worked up she gets, the more colorful her language becomes. I took another bite and leaned back in my chair. "People around here are

suffering and we're going to have to look that suffering in the eye.
It's a pustule that's about to pop." Suddenly, I wasn't so hungry.

I was beginning to understand that Steve and Suzanna's criticisms were critiques of our larger economic and cultural system and
not so much of Hardwick's agrepreneurial movement itself. Oh,
they had plenty to say about it, too, but even those concerns were
based largely on the degree to which particular operations or individuals had aligned themselves with traditional American business
tenets of achieving prosperity. And partly, I found myself simply
agreeing with them on many counts. To be sure, much of my acced-
ing to their rather radical view of things was stoked by my reporting
on this story. The global economy is crumbling at every corner, and
the financial system on which it is based lays in smoldering ruins.
What were these things built on? Um, let's see . . . oh yeah, that's it:
growth and profit. Greed. Entrepreneurialism. The four pillars of
American economic might, all of which balance rather precariously
on a single mast: consumerism. To think that we should maybe, just
maybe, consider a different way forward for our economic system—
just as we must for our food system—feels, at the end of the first
decade of the 21st century, like particularly sage advice.

The question that deserves to be asked, of course, is this: If
Steve Gorelick and Suzanna Jones don't like what they see happening in Hardwick, what *do* they like? They know the industrial food
system is dying on its synthetically fertilized, GMO-propagated
branch; they, as much as anyone, recognize the ills both physical
and communal (and, if you're willing to get even a little new-agey,
spiritual) it visits upon us. Wouldn't they like to see a Hardwick
food system prosper, even if it means lining the pockets of a handful of agrepreneurs? Wouldn't they like to see the creation of good
jobs with fair wages in an industry that should, at least in theory,
prove resilient to the forces of the broader economy?

Well, no, as it turns out: They wouldn't like to see these things.

The more we talked, the more it became clear that they want to see something far more seismic, something that would require nothing less than a total remaking of our culture and economy in ways that are at once compelling and also rather frightening to anyone who's become accustomed to enjoying a few hours of weekend leisure after a long week at his or her job in, say, advertising. Or perhaps race-car suspension tuning. "There are six billion people on this world," Suzanna said, channeling Vandana Shiva. The lasagna had been decimated; I was in the throes of a cheese-and-meat-induced stupor but she didn't seem fazed in the least (maybe she'd drugged me after all). "The only way six billion mouths can be fed is if 12 billion hands are allowed to work to produce the food."

"Well, I don't know about that . . . ," Steve tried to interject, but Suzanna was on another roll. There would be no interjecting.

"What these guys are doing in Hardwick is creating their own little empire, and it's not going to be anything different from a corporation owning the town. It's just guys with capital mediating between us and our needs. It's not an opportunity for us; it's being *imposed* on us. They talk about food security . . . I *hate* the term 'food security.' It's a fear term. It gets people all worked up." She pitched her voice high and nasal. "'Oh, my god, I need a blankie.' People come up with their own adaptations. That's one positive thing I can say about Americans: We adapt. We've done it before and we'll do it again. We don't need a bunch of white guys with money telling us how to adapt." She paused. Steve and I breathed. "God. People are always doing stupid things in the name of groovy ag movements."

I'd expected to leave Steve and Suzanna's feeling more conflicted than ever about Hardwick's agrepreneurial revolution, but as it turned out, I simply didn't have it in me. I'd already spent an enormous amount of time and energy trying to see the issue from every angle and trying to decide which view I should align myself with. This is the antithesis of objective, impartial journalism, but at this point, there wasn't much that was objective or impartial about my involvement in this story. I felt compelled to choose a side; Hardwick was part of my extended community, and Steve and Suzanna, the Toms, and everyone involved were friends or, at the very least, friendly acquaintances. And it didn't help that some people were pushing me to stake out a position: Early in my reporting, when Suzanna Jones was still hedging over whether or not she'd allow me to include her in this book, I'd explained that her ideas and critiques were an important part of the conversation surrounding Hardwick's food system. "Well, maybe you could just have those ideas yourself," she said. She wasn't joking.

But as much as Suzanna might want me to claim ownership of certain ideas about the Hardwick agrepreneurial movement, I can't. Much of what Steve and Suzanna have to say resonates with me. I can imagine what they imagine; I find it compelling to consider a society where individuals take personal responsibility for feeding themselves, where the purchasing power of the dollar has been usurped by that of radishes and rutabagas or the simple ability and willingness to work the soil in equality and dignity, where communities are stronger than corporations. And I have to chuckle at their specific criticisms of Hardwick's agrepreneurs, mostly because the images they conjure in delivering those criticisms are so devastatingly accurate. "The last thing Hardwick needs is Tom Stearns pacing up and down Main Street, blabbing on his cell phone," said Suzanna, and I could remember at least two specific instances when I'd watched him do exactly that. Or: "This whole thing is ego-driven. It's all about the attention they're getting." And the next day, I'd get an e-mail from Stearns telling me about all the interviews he had scheduled, about all the invitations he'd gotten to speak at various conferences of farmers and community leaders. Or: "All they care about is getting richer and bigger," and I'd think about Pete Johnson shopping for more land, a bigger tractor, another greenhouse.

At one point during one of our debates concerning the appropriateness of all of this, Suzanna made what I thought was a particularly salient point. "It's not so much that what they're doing is wrong," she said. "It's just that it's wrong for Hardwick. If they were doing this in Newark, New Jersey, it would be a great thing. They'd be moving in the right direction. But we already have the beginning of something else, something that's truly local." What she was saying is that it's not so much where you're at, but where you're going. Or a combination of the two. The scale on which you must measure the appropriateness of agricultural enterprises isn't static; it's comparative. Newark, New Jersey, doesn't have what Hardwick has had since long before Tom Stearns and his towering ambition to reinvent our food system moved in. In Newark, there is no Buffalo Mountain Food Co-op, no Forrest Foster and Karen Shaw. There are no Steve Gorelick and Suzanna Jones. In Newark, there is only one model to choose from, only one trough from which to feed, and it is the one that now finds itself on shaky footing. In such a context, it's hard to imagine an agricultural enterprise that wouldn't be a vast improvement on the status quo: Pete Johnson could pull on a 10-gallon hat, saddle up a 200-horsepower tractor, and turn over 300 acres, all in the name of small-scale, decentralized agriculture. Tom Stearns could make his millions, seed the city with a dozen ag-based start-ups, and it could rightly be heralded as a blow to corporate ag. In other words, the measure of a local food system is only partly the system itself. You have to judge local food systems in the context of where they are. By this reckoning, a healthy food system will always be the one that's moving toward the lower end of whatever scale is adequate to keep the locals nourished, spiraling toward the shortest, least-complex supply chain necessary to ensure that food reaches table. And finally, the appropriateness of any agricultural endeavor can't be measured merely against the extremely poor health of our industrial food system, it also must be measured against whatever alternatives already exist.

"The question we should be asking ourselves is not 'Is this better?' but 'What could there be?'" said Steve Gorelick as we sat around his dinner table that night. In a rare moment, Suzanna had ceded control of the conversation. "If all we're going to do is measure our progress against the extreme of industrial ag, we'll never realize our true potential. There's a whole other picture on the table, but it's almost like we're trying not to see it."

I think he's right, and I know that the criticisms voiced by Steve Gorelick and his wife have sharpened and expanded my thinking on the issues related to food and economic systems. They have much to offer. But let's be honest: We are all—and this includes Steve Gorelick and Suzanna Jones, with their solar panels, milk goats, and wood-burning cookstove—cogs in the wheel of our capitalist economy. We all deal in US currency, we all pay taxes, we all consume goods and services that were produced by for-profit corporations with little regard for the world beyond their balance sheets. To be sure, Steve and Suzanna do this less often and more thoughtfully than probably 99.9 percent of their fellow countrymen and countrywomen. But the fact remains: Just like the vast majority of Hardwick's 3,200 residents, they rely on an income paid in US currency to sustain them.

The families living in Hardwick's town center, in those old Victorians literally built on granite (the foundations of many of the homes in Hardwick are constructed of hulking blocks of the stone) and figuratively (granite-industry wages paid for many of these houses), with their quaint wooden shutters, fading paint, and splintered porches, still depend on a supply chain that extends far beyond their own small landholding, and that of their neighbors. They still depend on an economy that recognizes the exchange of money for food and labor as a legitimate trade, and they still depend on jobs to provide that money. During one particularly fevered rant, Suzanna had described the employment opportunities offered by Hardwick's agrepreneurs as "wage slavery." Perhaps that is true, but if so, it seems a kinder, gentler version of the wage slavery most of us are indentured to. Laboring in exchange for the money needed to acquire the goods necessary to sustain human life is an arrangement that predates our current food and economic predicaments by hundreds of years. Has it been corrupted by corporate interests? Why, yes, it has. Is the only answer to that corruption the wholesale abandonment of this model, with all the societal havoc such a transition would surely wreak? I don't believe it's quite that simple.

It is easy and satisfying to moralize about the capitalist model. It is easy and satisfying to draw those hard lines, not in the least because we get to assign the values to either side of that line and to decide which side to call our own. But is it really that uncomplicated? Because you can't just close your eyes and conjure an economy of food and labor exchange, where the banks accept carrots and cauliflowers in lieu of traditional dollar-denominated mortgage payments. Hardwick's citizenry still need jobs and the money those jobs bring in, and those jobs depend on businesses that can thrive while operating within the status quo. Is it too much to ask that these businesses explore ways in which they might begin the long, hard work of rewriting the metrics by which we measure progress? No, that does not seem like too much to ask. Is it too exacting to hold these businesses to a more stringent standard that favors employees with livable wages, pleasant working conditions maybe a side of pork and a couple cords of seasoned hardwood? No, that does not feel like too much. But to dismiss these businesses and individuals outright because they still hew to traditional business frameworks as they also endeavor to provide the regional citizenry with employment opportunities that fall outside of many of the common options in a rural, working class community? Well, yeah, that *does* seem like a bit much.

For his part, Tom Stearns isn't quite willing to simply dismiss the criticisms leveled against him. "People think I'm a media whore," he told me, and I nodded because, yes, some people do think that. "Maybe they're right. But by putting myself in that position, I'm inviting scrutiny. Hell, I *want* scrutiny. It might help me keep from getting carried away, because that happens sometimes." I nodded again. "I wish that anybody who doesn't like what we're doing would come visit High Mowing, or Pete's Greens, or whoever. Because, so far, they haven't. They've got a voice in the process, they've got a place at the table, if they want it. But frankly, I think they're happier standing on the sidelines, throwing stones."

Regarding the economic worthiness of Hardwick's agrepreneurial revolution, Stearns is a bit more direct. "Holy mackerel. How could anyone complain about us bringing good jobs to this community? I mean, geezum crow. We're talking about $14,000 per capita [the annual Hardick income]. We could do with a little, don't you think?"

I have empathy and respect for Steve and Suzanna. The honesty and passion of both their critiques and what they've created for themselves on their 40 bucolic acres could not be clearer. And I can imagine that if my little town of Cabot suddenly started appearing in the national media courtesy of a small group of ambitious entrepreneurs, I'd be pretty damn nervous and maybe a little suspicious. I'd probably find plenty of reasons to distrust. "It's not so much that I find the Hardwick 'movement' disagreeable," Gorelick told me. "It's that an already-existing movement has been taken over by people who are primarily entrepreneurs and businesspeople. I don't believe these people should be excluded from the table in some way, but it makes me uncomfortable to see them determining the direction this movement takes."

Still, I think Stearns makes a fine point: Thus far, the most vocal of his critics seem unwilling or simply uninterested in coming to the table themselves. They've staked out a position and are holding fast. But egalitarianism, equitability, and humility do not arise from one side meeting another's conditions; they come of both sides meeting each other's conditions or, at least, endeavoring to do so. We can tell ourselves all the stories we want: that our side of the line is just and right, that it's the only way forward. But in a complex society built on complex systems, the journey forward will always be more nuanced than that. To pretend that it won't be is to engage in self-delusion, and it occurs to me that we've been deluding ourselves for far too long already.

I never expected to become so embroiled in the moral aspects of food, and I'd begun to realize that to truly understand what was happening in Hardwick, to comprehend its implications for the town and, for that matter, anyone dependent on a global food system in crisis, I'd need to dig deeper. A lot deeper. And in a sobering way, I'd begun to feel a sense of responsibility that was bigger than what I'd felt about just telling a story that was entertaining and factually correct. Part of this was my own sense that I'd failed to fully grasp the story in my first go-round; if the media had truly done a disservice to the building of a movement that could prove critical to literally millions of people, then I needed to shoulder some of that blame for stoking the fires and driving the wedge. These were my neighbors; this was my community.

And there was this: By inserting myself into a hot-button issue in such a small community, I'd become part of the story I was reporting on. All the time spent with the Toms (Gilbert and Stearns),

Andrew Meyer, Pete Johnson, Forrest Foster and Karen Shaw, Mateo Kehler, Linda Ramsdell of the Galaxy Bookshop, Kristina Michelsen and bartender Don from Claire's, Steve Gorelick and Suzanna Jones, and so many others, was deeply affecting. Because, well, I *liked* these people. At the outset of this project, I'd assumed my proximity and connections to Hardwick would be to my advantage. But now I wasn't so sure. Objectivity and the cozy degree of insulation it provides were disappearing as fast as Iowa topsoil in a windstorm.

I know: This should have been obvious at the outset. I mean, why wouldn't I like these people? We've all chosen to live in the same area, for many of the same reasons. We share much in common. We think about food and food systems. We like to eat. Many of us have young children. We worry about the future of our country and therefore about the future of our kids. We grow gardens and keep chickens. We shop at the farmers' market and the co-op. We live in modest houses that we heat with wood. We go sledding in the first snowfall and curse the blackflies in spring. We see something in Hardwick, despite all its quirks and rough edges, that makes us want to live here or shop here or just be here. That makes us want to see it succeed, according to a notion of success that is either clarified and secured or obscured and threatened by the town's emergence as food system savior. This is the glaring divide that challenged me, and it doesn't help that some feel as if this "emergence" is being foisted upon them and perpetuated by the media and certain people—but not others—in the community. "One of the beauties of this place is that it's always been ignored," said a friend. She had not been excited to hear I was writing this book. "I guess it's not being ignored anymore."

CHAPTER NINE

I rolled into the dooryard of Ralph and Cindy Persons at 6:45 on a clear, cold December morning. It was still half-dark; the lights in the house glowed through the windows and wood smoke curled from the chimney. A big Chevy pickup was idling in the driveway.

I already knew Ralph and Cindy pretty well. I met them in 1998, the first year we raised pigs on our small farm. Ralph and Cindy operate a mobile slaughtering service; in other words, they make their living killing animals. In most places, even in rural Vermont, finding someone to slaughter a couple of pigs would prove a daunting task; in our case, I needed only to ask a neighbor. "Call Ralph and Cindy," he said. "They're the ones you want."

The Personses reside in an aging farmhouse on the outskirts of Hardwick; they have a few acres of hilly land, upon which they run a menagerie of fowl (chickens, ducks, geese, peacocks) and mammals (horses and pigs, mostly). They are both on the wrong side of 50, and the deep creases in their faces make it clear it hasn't been a half-century of leisure. Until recently, they smoked Swisher Sweet cigars regularly. Giving up the Swishers may or may not have exacerbated their habit of gently bickering as they work: "Hey, that's my knife!" "No, it's mine!" "Hold that damn stomach open!" "I'm trying, I'm trying!" They love to gamble and frequently point their Chevy pickup south for the 6-hour drive to Foxwoods Casino in Connecticut. They make their own wines and brandies, typically from fruits and flowers they've gleaned from customers or gathered in the wild. I've been to their house a few times, and I've sampled from dark bottles containing various forms of home-brewed alcohol: pumpkin and dandelion wine, peach and apple brandy. Unlike much of the home-brewed alcohol I've drunk in my adult years, the Personses' is actually palatable and not something you'd drink simply because of what it does to your central nervous system. Ralph has one favorite joke that I've heard probably a dozen times: "So I get a call from this guy who wants me to come over and do a big ole steer, but he needs it done *right now*. So I say to the guy, 'What, you think I got time to kill?'" This is followed by the deep, moist chuckle of a man who was probably wise to give up smoking. Ralph grew up only a few miles from my childhood home in Maple Corner; for a time during my early high-school years, he was my bus driver.

Ralph and Cindy are gentle and patient teachers. From them I have learned how to cook pig liver, how to wrap fish in caul fat, and how to make a rich stock of chicken heads and feet. From them I have learned where to shoot a steer so that he drops in one swift *whump* and how to separate the hide from the carcass so that it remains whole and unblemished. It's always seemed to me that Ralph and Cindy Persons are emblematic of the town they call home. They are tough and independent, kind and proud, and they have been the way they are for so long, it's hard to imagine they could be another way. Do people make a town, or does a town make its people? It's some of each, probably, and both reinforce each other until a town's destiny shapes that of its residents, even as their future determines what will become of their town.

Ralph answered my knock, coming to the door wearing his trademark brown leather Stetson hat; the hair showing beneath it was almost pure white. Cindy was in the kitchen pouring coffee; she's thin, vivacious, and clever. Tough, too: A few days earlier, she'd shot a coyote and was planning to have the animal's front half mounted in an aggressive stance, with a half-snarl across its face. Their two small dogs twisted and twirled around my feet.

The Personses were eager to get going. On the day I joined them, they had five pigs and one steer scheduled for demise. Not a huge day, but for the hogs, we'd have to drive all the way to Stowe, about 30 miles to the west. For the steer, we'd return to Hardwick, hopefully by lunchtime. Ralph had polished off a quarter of an apple pie for breakfast, but Cindy hadn't eaten, so she grabbed a bottle of Mike's Hard Lemonade (for later, she assured me) and a couple slices of cold pizza and we hopped into the truck.

It is my belief that Ralph and Cindy Persons have done more for their town's food security, quality, and accessibility than anyone else. This may not be immediately clear; after all, Ralph and Cindy don't actually grow food for others. (This is not quite true: They do sell some broiler chickens and ducks, as well as live chicks and ducklings. And they provide hogs for the half-dozen or so pig roasts they do each summer, usually at weddings. But the thrust of their livelihood does not involve food production.) They don't operate a storefront, where food is sold or traded. They don't hire employees. They don't even *talk* about local food, at least not in the sort of highbrow language that's become so common. To them, the food system in which they play a pivotal role is just the way it's always been, the way it should be. Clearly, they are not local food purists. They're aware that their hometown has gotten press recently, but they haven't paid much attention. When I asked them if it meant anything to them, they just shrugged.

What the Personses do, more than anyone I've met in Hardwick or anywhere else, is enable people to raise their own food. They aren't so much slaughterers as they are enablers. They possess skills and equipment that have largely been lost to our society, and they make them available to their neighbors at a very reasonable price. For $50, Ralph and Cindy will come to your home, shoot your pig in the head, make a deep slice in its throat to sever the jugular veins, hoist it into the air (it's helpful but not essential to have a tractor with a bucket loader), skin it, remove its viscera (it's your responsibility to dispose of these bits; many of their customers compost the remains), and saw it neatly in half. Don't have a pig? They probably know where you can get one. They charge $2.75 for each chicken they slaughter, and $80 for a cow. If these do not seem like bargain prices to you, I promise it's only because you haven't performed these particular acts yourself.

The tools of Ralph and Cindy Personses' trade have a functional, unapologetic aesthetic. There were two guns in the truck, a .22-caliber rifle and .45-caliber handgun. Beside the guns sat a variety of hooks; two were S-shaped with points at either end. These would be used to hang the animals from a large, medieval-looking triangle of weathered steel called a gambrel. The other hook emerged, pirate-like, from a handle. This one was for dragging the hogs from where they fell to where they'd be dressed. It would also be used for the frequent prying and moving of large slabs of meat the work demands. There was a leather glove in the toolkit; it also contained a variety of knives and a long, round piece of steel for honing the blades, each stuck into its own glove finger. Coiled into a corner of the truck bed like a snake lay a chain, from which the gambrel would hang. There were a few other things, too, but these were the critical components of the day's business. In summer, when the Personses' business revolves around chickens, they tow a converted livestock trailer that contains a row of metal slaughtering cones into which the birds are placed upside down, with the head and neck projecting from the bottom for easy access with a knife; a large pot to be filled with hot water for loosening feathers; a motorized tub plucker that spins the birds like a hot-rod merry-go-round to separate them from their feathers; and a sink for evisceration. Last summer, Ralph and Cindy processed 22,000 birds. That is not a typo.

We wheeled through Hardwick, taking a left at the blinking light onto Route 15. There was little traffic. Ralph drove and Cindy rode in the cab's small rear seat, having ceded the front passenger seat to my gangly limbs. Ralph drove slowly and talked as we made our way west, the sun slowly rising behind us over the town's nearly silent streets. He spoke of the Iraq war (he is a Vietnam veteran, and he and Cindy have a son-in-law currently serving in Iraq), and he talked about their customers. He pointed to a house as we rolled by. "I've been doing her birds for 14 years. I've gone through the stages of watching her kids grow up and come back home. You know, they say this war is raising hell, but it's really making people think in new ways." The precise connection between these two statements wasn't immediately clear, but as I chewed it over, I began to understand. It was Ralph's way of saying exactly what I said at the outset of this book: Things are changing, and people are beginning to take notice. They're raising their own meat; their kids are coming home after college to settle in the community or even on the family homestead. The future will be different from the past.

We arrived at the home of Christine Kaiser shortly before 8:00. It was still cold, and our breath plumed. The pigs were beyond a rickety fence, behind the barn that houses Kaiser's 125 dairy goats. Christine's son, Clyde, was messing with the fence, which looked in danger of collapsing on itself. Christine, a short woman with a farmer's pragmatic bearing, came out of the barn. Cindy sent her to the house for a bucket of hot water.

I had observed the slaughtering of enough animals, and slaughtered enough myself, to know that there is a moment in the process where every movement and sound seems infused with the cold reality of what is about to transpire. This was that moment. Christine had returned with the bucket of water, and it sat steaming on the ground; the gambrel was hung from a chain attached to the bucket of a skid steer, a small loader. Ralph was reaching for his rifle with his right hand; in his left, he held the long blade he'd use to sever the pig's jugular veins. This is a tricky undertaking, because to ensure a good bleed, it's critical to cut through the veins quickly, while the heart is still pumping. Animals that aren't bled properly tend to have a gamey flavor and will be riddled with blood clots that must be cut out of the meat. But pigs are kickers; no matter how perfect your aim, no matter how quickly they crumple to the ground, they'll kick and thrash for a minute or more. Sticking an eight-inch blade into the precise spot where the jugular veins cross each other on their path from the heart to the body is hard enough without defending yourself against the death throes of a 300-pound animal.

Killing animals is not particularly fun, but there is a certain adrenalized anxiety to the process that I find strangely compelling. Is it the power that comes of wielding a loaded gun with clear intent? I'd like to think it's not, but I can't be certain. Guns are strangely beautiful pieces of machinery: There's the warmth of a smooth wooden stock juxtaposed against the polished chill of the barrel. And all those intricate parts, making their soft snicking sounds as you chamber a bullet or eject the clip or advance the chamber. It's the sound of precision in an imprecise world. I've never shot for sport, for the sole pleasure of pulling the trigger time and again, but I can understand the attraction. It's an extraordinarily visceral experience.

Some of the appeal, I think, is the depth of responsibility, not just to the animal, but to the simple act of feeding yourself and your family. We've created a system that demands almost no engagement with our food; we've wrung all the responsibility and sweat equity from the process. It's not that we're getting something for nothing; after all, we do pay for our food, and we suffer the consequences of dining from the industrial trough. But charging a package of center-cut pork chops to your Visa is a hell of a lot different than facing down the source of those chops with a .22 in one hand and a well-honed knife in the other.

Or maybe it's all merely the relief that comes from completing the process quickly, with the least possible disruption. That probably sounds absurd—after all, the goal is to effect the ultimate disruption—but there's a broad emotional chasm between a clean, one-shot kill to the brain and a head-shot pig that's running in wild, panicky circles. I know. I've been on both sides of that divide.

I'd be surprised if Ralph and Cindy still experience this; they've killed thousands of animals in 14 years of professional slaughtering. They go about their work in the pragmatic style of people measuring their actions against metrics of efficiency, profit, and customer satisfaction. The sort of emotional surges I experience during slaughter simply demand too much energy to sustain on a day-in, day-out basis.

Indeed, this is how it played out at the farm of Christine Kaiser. Ralph would shoot a pig, hand the rifle to Cindy, then scurry into the pen to slit its throat, the remaining ambulatory hogs scampering around him. Pigs don't seem to understand the death of a fellow swine; they'll typically react to the gunshot with some surprise, then sneak in for a sniff and prod at their departed brother before returning to their primary concern, which is, of course, eating. I've seen this play out again and again, and it occurs to me that this disinterest in death might be something of a blessing, particularly when it might well be your turn next.

With the pig shot and bled, I'd drag it over to the skid steer by jamming the meat hook through the bottom of its mouth, an act that felt horribly violent despite what had just taken place. Then I'd make two slits in the hind legs and slide an S-hook through each. (I was trying to be useful, and Ralph and Cindy were kind enough to allow me to believe that I was actually helping.) The upper

halves of the S-hooks were slung over the gambrel, and Clyde
would raise the pig so that its underside was exposed and its back
end hung at head height. While Ralph and Cindy readied their
knives, I sprayed the hog with a garden hose to remove any manure
that had stuck to it during the killing process. Then it was time to
cut. The whole process, from gunshot to butcher-ready halves,
took about 30 minutes per pig.

The Personses like to banter as they work and tell campy jokes,
particularly Ralph. For instance, after removing the feet from a pig
he'd just shot, Ralph turned to me and said, "Just want to make
sure he doesn't go anywhere." When Cindy went into the barn to
pee into the manure gutter, Ralph called to her: "The third goat
on the right is the friendly one." Cindy took this in stride, flipping
him the bird as she ducked around the corner.

About halfway through the third hog, Clyde trotted across the
road and returned with his 10-month-old daughter, whom he takes
care of while his wife is at work. (Clyde operates a small auto-repair
shop next to the goat barn; his wife is a nurse.) He propped her on
a folding lawn chair and she watched with enormous eyes and a
bemused expression. The pig was dangling from the gambrel,
about eight feet from her face. Ralph called over to her, "Ready for
lunch?" Cindy reached into the bed of the truck and retrieved a
can of Chelada, a Bud Light and Clamato concoction she calls
"breakfast beer." She handed it to Christine, who chugged it down
and signaled her approval.

By a few minutes after ten o'clock, all five pigs had been slaughtered and lay in the back of Christine's pickup truck, steaming in
the cold. She'd drive them to a butcher in northern Vermont, then
distribute the meat to her customers, most of whom had purchased
half a hog. In Vermont, anyone can sell meat by the whole, half, or
quarter; the customer is expected to purchase the animal live, at
which point he or she assumes full responsibility for the safety of

the meat. Customers could come to the farm and slaughter it themselves and butcher it in their kitchens, or they could do what most
purchasers of farm-raised meat do and assign those responsibilities
to the farmer, who will typically do exactly what Christine Kaiser
did: Call Ralph and Cindy Persons and schedule a slot with a local
meat cutter. Animals processed in this fashion cannot be sold as
individual cuts in a retail outlet (grocery or restaurant) because
they haven't been slaughtered in a federally inspected facility. The
customer never actually sees the animal alive; the first meeting
takes place at the butcher's, when the consumer picks up a few
boxes of wrapped meat stamped "not for resale."

As we packed up, Ralph relayed his recipe for pig liver to Clyde
(Vidalia onions, bread crumbs, and bacon, if you're wondering
what to do with yours), who stood with a fresh specimen in his
hands, looking entirely unsure of whether or not he wanted to be
standing under a cold December sun with a hot pig liver in his bare
palms. Because only a single customer had wanted a liver and they
couldn't convince Christina and Clyde to take any more, Ralph and
Cindy had procured a fresh one for their dinner. It lay in the open
bed of the truck, ensconced in a plastic bag. We finished packing
up, said our good-byes, and hopped into the truck. Cindy stuck a
few Molson Ices into the same small cooler that held the Mike's
Hard Lemonade and tucked into a piece of cold pizza. The Personses had earned $250 for a bit more than two hours of work,
which seemed like a pretty good deal. And Christine Kaiser had
paid $250 (or more specifically, her customers had paid; most farm-
ers pass along the slaughter fee) to have five pigs slaughtered and
halved, which seemed like a really, really good deal.

I wasn't exactly sure how many people had purchased pork
from Christine, but it was surely at least five or six. Which means
that Ralph and Cindy Persons, in their own quiet, unassuming
way, had just played a critical role in feeding half a dozen local

families. As we rolled through the upscale resort town of Stowe,
clad in boots splashed with pigs' blood, I wondered how many
communities in this country have access to the sort of skills I'd just
seen put to work. Maybe it was more than I imagined, but I doubted
it. Even in Vermont, there is more demand for on-farm slaughter
and custom meat processing than can be met. During the summer
and fall months, the Personses work six days per week, and the few
meat cutters that remain in business are almost constantly overwhelmed. I wondered what will happen when Ralph and Cindy
retire (he's 62; she's a decade younger). They aren't the only mobile
slaughtering service in Vermont, but they're almost certainly the
best known and busiest. Maybe as the food crisis intensifies and
it becomes ever clearer that business as usual won't suffice, there
will be a surge in the ranks of on-farm slaughterers. Maybe the
crumbling economy will prove a catalyst.

That's a lot of "maybes" in one paragraph, and I suppose it
reflects my concern that Ralph and Cindy Persons aren't just
unique in character, but in aptitude, too. They are a powerful antidote to our decaying industrial food system, but they are only two
people in a Chevy pickup stocked with guns and knives, pig liver
and pizza, Molson and Mike's, up against the corporate, profit-
driven model that holds us all hostage. I'm dramatizing, of course,
but not by nearly as much as you might like to think. The truth is
that if our country is going to truly escape the bounds of its over-
wrought food system, it will need tens of thousands of Ralph and
Cindy Personses, and it's hard not to ask the obvious question:
Where will they come from? Who will teach them the trade?

I left Ralph and Cindy's shortly after lunchtime; the steer had
gone as smoothly as the pigs and by noon, they were ready to call it
a day. We popped the caps on a few Molsons and ate more cold Pizza
Hut pizza, then Cindy loaded me up with bottles of home-brewed

dandelion and strawberry-rhubarb wine. The sun had finally thawed the day, and I drove home with the window down a few inches in deference to my boots, which smelled of dead pig.

As I drove, I thought about the tension surrounding the recent flurry of ag-related businesses and hyperbole in Hardwick, and I considered how it was that Ralph and Cindy hadn't become embroiled in that tension and why they probably never would. It wasn't because they weren't entrepreneurs; they'd seen an opening, filled a niche, and capitalized on it. What could be more entrepreneurial than that? And it wasn't because they didn't want to make money; after all, I'd just seen them make nearly $400 before lunch. Not bad, and on average probably a good bit more than any of the other ag-related business owners in the region make. Best of all, no one could reasonably argue that they charged too much.

No, what Ralph and Cindy Persons have going for them is their utter lack of pretense and their disinterest in being part of a movement. They are barely aware of what Tom Stearns and Andrew Meyer and all the other members of Hardwick's emerging agricultural economy are up to; they hadn't read the article in the *New York Times* or dined at Claire's. They don't market themselves; they don't have a Web site or an ad in the Yellow Pages or even a sign on their truck. They've been doing what they do for so long, they've become an entity unto themselves, an example of something that works because it works, not because it's "local" or "organic" or "sustainable." In a way, they remind me of my grandfather, who farmed his whole life without ever really articulating the values of his profession or its place in the larger fabric of his life.

It occurred to me again that much of the emerging tension hinged less on what the new crop of agrepreneurs was doing than on what they were saying they were doing. If they'd just kept their mouths shut and kept doing what they'd always done, or kept doing what they'd just started to do until it seemed like the thing they'd always done, perhaps they wouldn't have attracted so much attention.

Beyond their obvious allure as characters, this is why I find Ralph and Cindy so appealing. They simply do not care whether what they do fits within the framework of the local food trend. They don't tailor their message or attempt to somehow soft-pedal the grisly nature of their work. They carry pig livers home for dinner in the bed of their pickup; they keep a bag of chicken feet for the dogs on top of the woodpile just outside their front door, right under the wind chimes. They were curious about why I was curious about them, but it was only a passing curiosity. If a healthy food system is one that's built from the ground up, on trial and toil and the humble willingness to do what needs to be done, even when what needs to be done might be difficult and dirty, then the Personses are as much a model of inspiration as anything that's happening in Hardwick. And they don't even know it.

Just before I left the Personses on that early December afternoon, with only an inch or two remaining in the second (or was it the third? I'm really not accustomed to drinking beer at noon) Molson of lunch, after Ralph had shown me the wristwatch he received from the Foxwoods Casino in appreciation of his frequent patronage, we started talking about food. It wasn't a serious discussion in the sense that it lacked the grandiosity of vision and sense of urgency I'd become accustomed to when talking food with the Toms, Andrew Meyer, Steve and Suzanna or, frankly, almost anyone with whom I broached the subject. In fact, I'm not even sure how we veered onto the subject (had we been talking about casino fare?), except that in Ralph and Cindy's world, food is never far from view, and it's usually covered with blood.

"I like to tell people little things," said Ralph. We were standing next to a table that held two hunting rifles and a meat saw. "Like how to cook heart so the whole family will love it, or make liver so their kids will eat it." He set his beer on the table. "I know it's just little things, but I think little things can make a difference."

I nodded my head dumbly, but what I was thinking, even through the fog of Molson and the waning tendrils of slaughter adrenaline, was just how profound those little things can be, how you can never be certain just what action or kindness will be the one that reaches something in a person that's never been reached before. There are so many ways to make this happen; there's no particular reason the vector should be food. But there's also nothing more appropriate. Food can be viewed as a metaphor for life, happiness, community, ritual, or pretty much anything you want. Or it can be viewed simply as a means to an end, as the fuel that enables us to greet another day.

Ralph Persons may have thought he was talking about little things. But no matter which view you prefer, he wasn't.

CHAPTER TEN

A food system, be it local, national, international, or intergalactic, doesn't run on goodwill and clear thinking alone. There are and always will be certain inputs needed to cultivate food, and those inputs are no less essential to the system's survival than oxygen is to yours and mine. In this sense, Hardwick is ahead of the game. After all, how many communities are home to an organic heirloom seed company? Most farmers—even those operating on the same principles that drive Hardwick's evolving system—buy seeds from hundreds, if not thousands, of miles away. And while it's true that High Mowing Organic Seeds purchases some of its stock from California and even Israel, it's also true that the company sources nearly a third of its seed from Vermont. The entire Hardwick region could conceivably be fed on food that grew from local seed.

Still, a seed without soil is about as useful as a piano on a submarine, and in this regard, Hardwick is again fortunate. "If Hardwick soils were in Iowa, they'd be farmed nonstop," Thomas Villars told me. Villars is a soil resource specialist with the USDA Natural Resources Conservation Service; he works from an office in White River Junction, Vermont, about 90 minutes south of Hardwick. "Most of them fall under the national criteria for prime farmland."

Broadly, Hardwick falls within two physiographic regions. (This is the term geology and soil wonks use to define geologic subdivisions based on terrain, rock type, and geologic history.) The town's western fringe marks the beginning of the Green Mountain region, where the land begins its run-up to the state-long spine of

3,000- to 4,000-foot peaks that comprise the Green Mountain range. The mountains themselves are, of course, entirely unsuitable for agriculture (at least of the lawful sort; a tremendous amount of high-grade marijuana is grown on the flanks of the Greens). But the expanse between Hardwick and the foothills, which extends almost 20 miles, is open and not terribly hilly. The soil types are Tunbridge and Lyman, and bedrock lurks not far beneath the surface. Tunbridge and Lyman aren't bad for farming; the vast majority of the world's farmers would kill for such rich earth.

Still, the really good stuff lies in the central and eastern parts of Hardwick, where a physiographic region called the Vermont Piedmont sweeps through on its stretch from Canada to Massachusetts. Here, the terrain is flatter (drive through the area and you'll understand that "flat" is a relative term), and the deep, rich soil rides on a foundation of stone known as the Waits River Formation. It's this bedrock, Villars explained, that lends Hardwick soil its unusual natural fertility and high pH. "The Waits River Formation has a lot of limestone and phyllite, which are high in calcium. The calcium leaches into the soil. It's very nourishing." I'd never before considered that stone could be a source of nourishment; I was beginning to realize how little I truly knew about soil and fertility.

This I did know: Plants grow by absorbing nutrients and water from the soil and taking chemical energy (which they use for photosynthesis) from the sun. There are 16 elements that are essential to plant growth, and by "essential," I mean that the nutrient element must be either directly involved in the metabolism of the plant or it is necessary for the plant to complete its life cycle. Nine of these elements are required in relatively large amounts: nitrogen, phosphorus, potassium, calcium, magnesium, sulfur, carbon, hydrogen, and oxygen. These are the macronutrients that make a plant grow.

The seven other elements are required in small, sometimes minute, quantities, and they are: iron, manganese, zinc, boron, molybdenum, copper, and chlorine.

The soils in eastern Hardwick are of four primary types: In the broad, lush pastures where cattle graze and hay ripens under summer sun, the soil type is Cabot; on the well-drained knolls, it's Buckland. Along the wide, fertile river bottoms, it's Charles and Podunk (yes, there really is a soil type known as Podunk). If you were casting about for a place to launch a small-scale, low-input agriculture operation, you probably couldn't do much better than to plop yourself in eastern Hardwick and commence to turning over a chunk of that bedrock-fed Podunk.

Of course, all this ignores Hardwick's obvious shortcoming, which can be reduced to roughly one word: winter. From about mid-October to mid-May, the weather in northern Vermont is a capricious and vengeful thing. By the end of September, a killing frost is pretty much guaranteed, and from there, you've got maybe a month before the first snow falls. Prime soils are all well and good, but if they're frozen to the consistency of steel or smothered beneath three feet of snow, there's not a hell of a lot you can do with them.

But in a way, it might just be that Hardwick's climatic limitations are helping to drive the nature of the region's agriculture. Because if Hardwick enjoyed the sort of year-round growing conditions of, say, California or Florida, it would likely be inundated with industrial-size ag operations driving up land prices, fouling the groundwater, and running the smaller operators out of town. Actually, it would probably have been like this for so long and the town would have evolved so differently that there wouldn't have been any small operators to begin with. The fact is, what's happening in Hardwick is very much suited to the unique confluence of natural advantages and deficits of the region. That's not to say that it couldn't be done anywhere else, only that here, perhaps more than any place in our vast nation, it makes perfect sense.

The first snow of the 2008 to 2009 winter fell right on schedule, on the night of October 28. Like most early snows, it was wet and heavy and started as rain in the daylight hours, drilling down onto Hardwick's streets and soaking deep into her soils, bending the tops of the soybean plants on Bridgman Hill, running down the wet flanks of thousands of cattle, and frothing the cold, steely surface of the Lamoille River. It let up late in the afternoon, then began again in earnest; at some point during the night, the temperature dropped into the low 30s, and the rain changed over to snow. By morning, the ground was white.

As usual, the transition to winter weather was sudden and shocking. The day before had been warm and golden in a way that suggests summer might never end. In mid-afternoon, I climbed the steep, narrow stairs to the offices of the Highfields Center for Composting to meet its director, Tom Gilbert. Highfields is headquartered in a pair of rooms above the Galaxy Bookshop, Hardwick's independent bookstore. The building originally housed a bank, which means the Galaxy is quite likely the only bookstore in the country with a drive-up story-telling window and retail space in a vault.

Gilbert is a scruffy-looking 30-year-old with a fondness for sweater vests and a laconic countenance that can't quite mask his simmering intensity. On the day I visited, he was dressed in a plaid shirt with leather elbow patches and, true to form, a gray sweater vest. We'd met a time or two previously, so he felt comfortable enough to greet me in his usual manner: "Hey, trouble." He was drinking tea from a ceramic mug; his blond hair sprouted in innumerable directions from beneath a well-worn baseball hat. We'd planned to meet at the office before driving up to the composting site, which is situated on a high ridge about three miles west of town. "Can I ride with you?" he asked. "I rode my bike to work today."

It's stunning to consider how little attention this country pays to the issue of soil fertility, particularly when one considers how critical it is to almost every facet of our lives. The United States is blessed with naturally rich soils; its role as breadbasket to the world wasn't awarded merely on the basis of its size. The topsoil in the midwestern United States is world-class, and the topography of the region—broad expanses of table-flat field—is ideally suited to agriculture.

Of course, we've done our best to destroy our national soil gift. The devastating Dust Bowl storms of the 1930s are sometimes blamed on drought, but the damage was actually inflicted in the years prior, with a frenzy of plowing and overgrazing that stripped the land of its ability to weather the dryness to come. Massive soil conservation efforts helped usher out the Dust Bowl era; by the time the rain started falling again in 1939, the dust storms had largely abated.

Just as we emerged from this soil emergency, we implemented another: The second coming of the American agricultural revolution began in the early '40s, and it was characterized by a sharp rise in the use of chemical fertilizers and mechanized farm machinery that dramatically boosted per-acre production. In the 1930s, commercial fertilizer use averaged 6,599,913 tons per year. From 1940 to 1949, it averaged 13,590,466 tons per year. On a percentage basis, it's the largest decade-to-decade increase in US history. Is it a coincidence that the last US president who seemed to understand the value of topsoil was Franklin Roosevelt? "A nation that destroys its soil, destroys itself," Roosevelt famously proclaimed in 1937. If he was right, we've got problems.

In any case, the widespread use of chemical fertilizer and mechanized farm implements raised the curtain on an entirely new farming paradigm. It must have seemed miraculous at the time; for generations, farming practices had been largely dictated by nature and the limits of human and animal power. Suddenly, farmers could sprinkle a little fertilizer, fire up the John Deere, and reap massive, never-before-realized yields. Agriculture had gone linear.

It may be a while before we recognize the true costs of this "revolution"; technology is still keeping us one step ahead of nature, but it becomes a slightly smaller step every year. The depth of Iowa's topsoil has been halved over the past 150 years, from 16 inches to 8, and the state loses approximately 12 tons of topsoil per acre per year. Meanwhile, the 174,000-square-mile Ogallala Aquifer, which provides the irrigation water for 27 percent of the United States' irrigated farmland, is being depleted at a rate of 12 cubic kilometers per year, even as we demand ever more of it. In 1950, it irrigated 3.5 million acres of farmland; today, it waters 16 million acres. The Ogallala is not an aquifer that "recharges" quickly; most of the water being pumped from the Ogallala is more than a million years old, and it is currently being drained at 10 times the rate of its natural recharge. Some experts believe it will run dry within 25 years.

These woes are due almost entirely to modern industrial agriculture techniques that simply wouldn't be possible without tremendous inputs of chemical fertilizer and diesel fuel. Monoculture, the practice of sowing the same crop in the same soil year after year, has stripped the soil of precious nutrients and undermined the complex ecology of the organisms and minerals necessary for soil health. This, in turn, has necessitated ever-increasing applications of fertilizer, which makes the whole fragile treadmill spin even faster, as the topsoil slowly disappears and the massive yields supported by the heavy doses of chemicals demand more and more water.

So far the results, at least when measured in the immediate terms of bushels per acre, have been impressive. Even as the depth and biologic diversity of our soil decreases, even as the aquifer that supplies more than one-fifth of US cropland is drained of its million-year-old bounty, our agricultural yields rise. Our nation's record corn harvest (so far) came in 2007, when farmers reaped a stunning 155.8 bushels per acre, with some regions reporting harvests in excess of 200 bushels per acre. New strains of genetically modified seed that can survive conditions that would kill off today's corn are being developed and have some predicting a doubling of yields within the next two decades. For a little perspective on these numbers, consider this: Prior to the widespread use of chemical fertilizers, mechanized farm machinery, and GMO seed, yields averaged 40 bushels per acre. The fact that we are reaping corn at a rate 300 percent higher than nature intended is surely a testament to our ingenuity. But it is just as surely a testament to our short-sightedness. The only question is: Which one will give way first?

Tom Gilbert trades in a very different model of soil fertility. That much was clear the moment we arrived at the composting site, which sits at the edge of a broad expanse of ridgetop farm field on Hard-wick's West Hill Road. The entire operation covers less than an acre; there were a small, shacklike office, a bucket tractor for flipping compost piles, and a pair of small concrete bunkers where livestock mortalities (or "morts") are laid and layered with other materials to decompose. Under ideal conditions, it takes less than three weeks for bacteria to consume the flesh of a 1,500-pound dairy cow. There were also a dozen or so piles of compost and compost feedstocks in varying degrees of decomposition. It was a cool day, but the air still smelled strongly of something rotting. It wasn't a bad smell, per se, but I didn't spend much time breathing through my nose, either, and I chose to believe that the odor was not of animal origin.

Highfields is a fairly new enterprise; it was founded in 1999 by
Tod Delaricheliere, a local dairy farmer who'd spent the previous
four years experimenting with composting the manure excreted by
his cows. There are numerous reasons to compost manure, rather
than applying it fresh. For one, the composting process literally
cooks the pathogens (*E. coli*, *Salmonella*) that could catch a ride on,
say, a head of lettuce and cause a potentially fatal illness. That's
why vegetable farmers never spread fresh manure. But even in circumstances where fresh manure can be applied (many farmers still
spread it on their hayfields, for instance), composting is preferable.
That's because nitrogen—the critical nutrient in crap—is extremely
volatile. It doesn't want to just lie there on your field, seeping con-
tentedly into the ground and nourishing the roots below the surface; it would far rather return to the atmosphere as a gas. Fresh
manure can lose as much as half of its nitrogen content within 12
hours of being spread.

As Gilbert explains it, the act of composting is really nothing
more than creating a nitrogen bank. Bacteria and fungi develop,
consuming nitrogen and storing it in their microscopic bodies as
protein. When one dies, it is cannibalized by its peers. With proper
management, it takes less than a month to convert a pile of unsta-
ble nitrogen and carbon into a finished pile of biomass. Spread on
a field, compost will release its nutrients over a period of years,
rather than hours and days. "Think of it as a time-release vitamin
for your soil," said Gilbert.

Gilbert began working at Highfields in 2000; a native of
Brooklyn, he'd begun to distance himself from his urban upbringing at an early age, courtesy of an uncle who cultivated corn, soy,
and wheat in rural Kansas. When Gilbert was 14, he spent a summer on his uncle's farm, and those months under the relentless sun
of the US breadbasket affected him profoundly. "It excited me so

much to be part of such a fundamental process, to be out in the field with heat lightning flashing all around us, harvesting wheat that was going to feed somebody," he recalled. "We used to dive into the bins of wheat. There was so, so much of it."

With 4,000 acres under cultivation, Gilbert's uncle was a commodity farmer on a scale that is massive even by today's inflated standards. But at the age of 14, young Tom wasn't thinking about issues of appropriate scale or how soil fertility might act as an agent for social change. Mostly, he was just fascinated by it all, and the immensity of his uncle's farm, with its endless waves of ripening food and barns full of machinery, was exactly the sort of tinder that fuels the adolescent imagination: "I certainly wasn't looking at it with a critical eye. In fact, I suspect it was the scale that got me so excited."

Unlike many of his peers in the business of large-scale ag, Gilbert's uncle spent a lot of time thinking about the future and sustainability of his operation. "For an industrial grower, he was a really innovative, thoughtful farmer," said Gilbert. "Even back then, he was thinking about water conservation. This was a time when the basic mantra was 'use your allotment or lose it.'" He was speaking of the complex, convoluted, and ever-evolving rules governing rights to the water in the Ogallala Aquifer, which irrigates most of the crops grown in Kansas. Recently, Gilbert's uncle received organic certification for his farm, and he now grows specialty wheat for King Arthur Flour.

Not long after Tom Gilbert's introduction to industrial agriculture, he convinced his parents to allow him to spend a summer at the family's vacation home in southern Vermont. While there, he worked on a vegetable farm, pulling weeds for 60 hours each week, using the mindless, repetitive nature of the task as an opportunity to think about localized agriculture and how it might offer the leverage necessary for community building. He carried those thoughts to Evergreen State College in Olympia, Washington, a progressive, liberal arts school that specializes in education and environmental studies.

"My personality is such that I don't arrive somewhere and stay too long without finding something to plug into," Gilbert told me. At Evergreen, that something was a zeal for small-scale ag, a broad focus that Gilbert soon narrowed to include a singular, almost obsessive passion: compost. He soon connected with a like-minded undergrad, a fellow named Jeff Klug. "At first, it was just the two of us reading journals, smoking joints, and masturbating on ideas."

From those humble roots, Gilbert and Klug designed an innovative hybridized composting system that utilized enclosed auto-venting concrete and steel containers called bioreactors and engineered worm bins known as continuous flow vermiculture reactors. In the simplest terms, the bioreactors would begin the composting process and the worms, through the magic of digestion and elimination, would finish it off. "The goal was to design a system that could fit on a community lot, that didn't have a massive footprint or odor issues. We wanted something that anyone in Brooklyn or Los Angeles or Oakland could implement."

To appreciate Gilbert's fervor for compost, it's crucial to understand that he views the substance as more than a means to add fertility to the soil. He considers compost an agent of social change. "One of my missions is to equip people with the tools for community health and sovereignty. I'm most interested in how whole systems can be used to combat other forms of oppression." I couldn't quite master the connection between rotting food and freedom from oppression, so I asked him to expand on the thought. "Compost is a really big stick with a lot of leverage. For starters, these systems can create good, sustainable jobs that are based on renewal and agriculture. And by holding onto these resources, a community begins to free itself from dependence on externalities like fertilizer. So much of our food system is based on nutrients from far away. Compost is a giant step toward sovereignty."

At first, Evergreen State College didn't see the connection, either. Gilbert and Klug petitioned the school to support their project. The school refused. "We had a blowout with the administration and basically said 'Fuck the school' and started a guerrilla composting system, with five-gallon buckets everywhere." Then the duo stumbled upon an abandoned building owned by Evergreen and centralized the operation. "At this point, we were getting really paranoid, because the school really wasn't happy with us. So we started composting at night." If ever there's an appropriate metaphor for our misplaced agricultural priorities, the image of two college students composting by headlamp for fear of being discovered seems to me like it might be it.

Eventually, through the time-honored practice of sheer, youthful persistence, Gilbert and Klug convinced the school to come on board. "They finally said, 'Okay, okay,' and we said, 'You know, there's this old building that'd be perfect for this.'" Now, the program is an Evergreen showpiece, part of the school's Center for Ecological Living and Learning.

From Evergreen, Gilbert moved on to the University of Maine Compost School and then, through happenstance, ended up in Hardwick working in the fields at Riverside Farm. He lived on the farm for two years with his wife, Molly, before accepting the Highfields position. He and Molly bought an unfinished house on 15 acres in Craftsbury and settled in.

There was plenty of work to do on the Craftsbury property, but one of the first tasks Tom Gilbert tackled was the construction of a custom flushless toilet so that he and Molly might compost their own feces and urine. "How many people look at their shit in the toilet and see it as something disturbing, something to dispose of as quickly as possible?" he asked me as we stood among the tall stacks of compost. He was looking at me expectantly, perhaps because he knew the answer and he knew I knew the answer, which was, of course: everybody.

"Everybody," I said, taking the bait.

He smiled, because he'd tricked me. "I've been composting my own crap for 12 years," he said. "It's almost a spiritual thing." He crossed his arms in a gesture of unpremeditated defiance, not toward me, I understood, but toward this entire culture of fecal ignorance, misplaced revulsion, and misappropriated priorities. "It's killing me not to be doing it right now." The latter comment referenced the recent sale of the Craftsbury property and the subsequent move, with his wife and two young children, to a rental home in Hardwick (complete with conventional flush toilet and septic) while they waited for the perfect farm to come on the market.

In addition to his position at Highfields, Gilbert serves as vice president of the Composting Association of Vermont and sits on the board of the Center for an Agricultural Economy. Despite the fact that he tends to speak in a thoughtful, wordy fashion that my friend Steve Gorelick dubs "the language of the nonprofit," Gilbert has become adept at paring down explanations of the art, science, and rationale behind composting to their layperson essentials.

"Most Americans don't understand what externalities are and they don't understand things they can't see." He pointed to a large, gray container sitting in the shade of the office building. "There's 48 gallons of organic nitrogen in that barrel. That's the equivalent of 58 gallons of natural gas." Natural gas is used in manufacturing synthetic nitrogen through what's known as the Haber-Bosch process, whereby nitrogen from the atmosphere (the air we breathe is 78.1 percent nitrogen) and hydrogen from natural gas react over an iron catalyst, creating ammonia, which is 82 percent nitrogen. Nearly 5 percent of global natural gas production is burned in producing nitrogen fertilizer. Written in chemists' terms, the Haber-Bosch process is this: $N_2(g) + 3H_2(g) = 2NH_3(g)$, $\Delta Ho = -92.4$ kJmol^{-1}.

In a sense, what happens at the Highfields Center for Composting is no less complex; one could write an algebraic equation for the composting process that would make Haber-Bosch look like grade-school math. But despite this, and despite Tom Gilbert's bemoaning our collective inability to grasp things we can't see, I'd argue that it's a hell of a lot easier to understand. That's because the monthlong process of converting feedstocks into field-ready compost is remarkably similar to the process of being human. In an active compost pile, bacteria are engaged in a constant feeding frenzy, noshing on the shit and flesh and vegetables and wood chips. The bacteria reproduce. They die. In other words, compost doesn't just sit there. It lives.

To bring it to life, the staff at Highfields must engage in some decidedly messy work. There are piles of manure to be moved and tubs of food scraps to be tossed. The deceased cows that arrive at the facility are often in the early stages of decomposition, with bloated stomachs that must be punctured before the animal can be added to the pile. This is not a pleasant undertaking. But mostly, making compost requires a basic understanding of process, a steady supply of feedstock, a knack for timing, and a willingness to wait.

As Tom Gilbert and I talked, I pressed my hand into a pile of the finished product. The center of an active compost pile can exceed 200°F (160°F is considered optimal), but at wrist depth it was soothingly warm and had a loamy, almost silky texture. I put a handful to my nose and inhaled. There was an odor, but it was not overpowering or unpleasant; the smell was at once lighter and more fully rounded than soil. It was one of those smells that resonates on your tongue, and it didn't taste bad, actually. I tried to imagine that what I was holding to my face had only a few weeks ago been cow shit and orange peels and leftover lasagna and even the cow itself; I tried to be repulsed by this. But the transformation had been as utter and complete as the seed that grows into a tomato plant or the sperm and egg that make a child.

I asked Gilbert if he ever gets discouraged that so few Americans understand the value of what he does. He shrugged. "I think we're closer than we know. I think there's a shared sense that something is awry right now." He again crossed his arms across his chest. "The greatest limitation is our expectations. They just get in the way of being very present with what's in front of us." I nodded, but I already knew it would take me a while to digest and consider all the ramifications of this.

The sun had nearly dropped behind the mountain peaks to our west, and it was getting cold. We hopped into my Subaru and drove back into Hardwick. The late-afternoon light played off the few leaves remaining on the maple trees that bordered the road. Five minutes later, parked along Main Street, across from the Highfields offices, we sat, watching the traffic roll past and chatting about what was happening in Hardwick. Gilbert seemed to harbor questions about the recent influx of agriculture-based businesses or, more to the point, about the expectations they had fostered. "There's a lot of hype right now, and I'm a little uncomfortable with it," he said. "We have not created a new food system in Hardwick; we're just rebuilding and utilizing an infrastructure that was already here. I think we let the media get ahead of us. People read that all this amazing stuff was happening, and it put everyone's expectations on steroids."

What Gilbert was reacting to, more than anything, was the

talk about things he didn't yet see happening. "Collectively, the new ag businesses have brought 75 to maybe 100 jobs to the area. That's a good start, but the reality is not born out of collective efforts. It's still individuals." And as we chatted in my Subaru on that cool fall evening following our visit to the composting site, he seemed leery of the relationship that was being built with the media (to be honest, he seemed leery of me). As a board member of the Center for an Agricultural Economy, Gilbert had a unique and not always enviable view of how the organization worked. "We sit in meetings and somebody farts and Tom Stearns is like, 'Someone call the *Gazette*, quick.'"

He sighed and settled back in his seat. "Sometimes, it just feels like too much." he says. "We need to just slow down. This is a building process, and we're not ready to put the roof on, because we haven't got the walls up."

CHAPTER ELEVEN

It was a warm, overcast afternoon, and the leaves on the sugar maples were glowing red and orange against the gray backdrop of the sky as I drove up a gravel road just west of Hardwick village. The road wound its way up the hill, past a long-abandoned farmhouse that looked out over the valley cleaved by Route 15, then bore left along a ridgeline. A half-mile later, I turned into one of the trial fields operated by High Mowing Organic Seeds, where the company develops and tests vegetable and fruit varieties with an eye toward their taste, hardiness, and germination rates.

Like most of High Mowing's cultivated acreage, this was leased land; Stearns leases 30 acres in the hills surrounding his company's Wolcott offices. He pays $40 per acre per year, which I found astonishingly cheap. Even in the midst of a real estate collapse, farmland in the Hardwick region was selling for upwards of $3,000 an acre. Renting land, therefore, is a common practice in the area, and the benefits flow both ways: Landowners can reap tax advantages while assuaging any guilt they might feel about letting their farmland lie fallow. The story of rural Vermont can't be told without acknowledging the tension between wealthy landholders who perch expansive homes in the midst of hundred-acre parcels they have no intention of farming and the farmers who can't afford to expand in an era of $3,000 acres.

Stearns was in the field when I arrived, walking alone down a long row of leafy plants. A few dozen feet away, a young woman on a tractor drove across a swath of dun-colored soil, dragging a disc harrow. The turned-over earth lent the air a dense, almost smoky aroma. Stearns was wearing his usual garb—field-dusted khakis, a wool vest, and a pair of battered hiking boots—and he was in his usual buoyant mood. He'd come to meet with Pete Johnson, the owner of Pete's Greens, to brainstorm techniques for collecting the pulpy flesh of the squash and pumpkin that remains after Stearns's employees extract the seeds. High Mowing generates nearly 500,000 pounds of the stuff each year; typically, it's left in the field to rot and fatten the neighborhood deer population. Stearns had accepted the waste for more than a decade; after all, it was the seeds he was harvesting, not the flesh. But his entrepreneurial mind was irked by the image of those towering piles of orange and yellow fermenting into the soil. There just had to be a way to convert the field waste to table food; there had to be a way to make some money off it. Johnson's operation, which includes an industrial kitchen and a full-time chef, seemed a logical next step. "I've been trying to crack this nut for a while," Stearns told me. "Pete's got this big-ass kettle, I think it holds like 500 pounds or something, and he's got this industrial pulper that'll just smash the bejesus out of 'em." He clearly relished the idea, and one of the things I was beginning to appreciate about Stearns was the childlike purity of this pleasure, which seemed to pop up everywhere. The fact that he could insert the terms "big-ass" and "bejesus" into the same sentence without even a whisper of irony didn't hurt, either.

Johnson was running late, so Stearns led me on a tour of the field, which looked to me like an oversize version of a home garden. I recognized carrots and lettuce and the remnants of tomato plants, but I didn't recognize a lot of things, including a purple-stalked plant with long, flower-topped stems emerging from its center like antennae. Stearns snapped off a stem and handed it to me. The yellow flower bobbed and weaved as I brought it to my mouth; the flavor was sweet and vaguely broccoli-ish, but with none of broccoli's stringy toughness. "It's hon tsai tai," explained Stearns. Then he added, unnecessarily, "It's not something most Anglos eat."

I found the trial field immensely appealing in much the same way that I'd been drawn to Nick and Taylor Meyer's dairy farm. The hard labor that had surely been invested was absent from my view (and the tractor driving looked pretty darn fun), and the broad variety of plants and their associated colors—green and purple and yellow—fit exactly within the framework of my notion of what localized agriculture should look like. The whole scene was strictly agrarian; there were no hard corners anywhere, no buildings or computers or cell phones (except for the one hanging dorkily from Stearns's belt). I could imagine awakening in the morning (in a small cabin, constructed of local materials and perched at the forest's edge to block the harsh winter winds) and strolling outside—still naked, for there were no neighbors in sight—to harvest my day's nourishment, and maybe enough for the neighbors I couldn't see, too.

A few minutes later, Johnson arrived, piloting a red Toyota pickup that was at least 15 years old and so obscured by mud that its license plates had been rendered illegible. His headlights wouldn't have done him a heck of a lot of good, either. Johnson opened his door and climbed out. It looked as if he'd dressed to match his truck: He was wearing tall rubber muck boots, dirty (and when I say "dirty," I mean *dirty*) blue jeans, and a similarly soiled Carhartt jacket. His fly was down. His hair (dirty blond, of course) was unruly to an extreme that should have been impossible without the benefit of an open-cockpit airplane.

Stearns and I hopped into Stearns's Subaru wagon and followed Johnson to an adjacent field. Two dogs, one Johnson's, one his girlfriend's, ran between the vehicles, tongues lolling, tails high in the air. The field was tilted slightly; we entered on the uphill side, and I caught a glimpse of the squash and pumpkin patch at its back edge, where dozens of bright orange cucurbits (the cucurbit family includes cantaloupes, gourds, pumpkins, squashes, and watermelons) blazed like small fires. In the middle of the field, next to one of the piles, a Chevy pickup was parked. One of Stearns's employees was hacking apart pumpkins with a broad axe; another was feeding the hewn slabs into an ominous-looking contraption the truck had towed there. It featured a hopper and a large, horizontally oriented drum that spun rapidly, rattling the seeds loose and allowing them to slip through its honeycombed sides. "That's our squash-seed extractor," Stearns told me proudly. "We designed it ourselves." The hunks of pumpkin bounced through the extractor and were spit onto the ground, where Johnson, Stearns, and I waited to paw through them, tossing the choice bits into the feed sacks Johnson had brought. "God, look at the material we're dealing with here," said Stearns, sounding as if he were sorting large, unmarked bills, not oozy bits of vegetable. "This is organic pumpkin, already grown, just rotting on the ground. We just need to find a market for it."

For a few minutes, but for the low rumble of the seed extractor, it was quiet. Johnson's kitchen manager arrived with a fresh stack of empty bags. We concentrated on the task at hand, and the bags slowly filled. The sun made a brief appearance, and I stripped down to my T-shirt. My fingers were slimy; the thick, almost-sweet smell of pumpkin was all around us. On one level, the task felt laborious and all but futile: We could stay in that field for days, hunched over and hot, and still not capture all of this tremendous bounty of food. But on another level, it felt deeply satisfying and important: After all, anything we gleaned was more than had been gleaned before. We were working the margins, getting something for almost nothing. A couple hours in a field, a little backache, some rendering in Johnson's big-ass kettle, and people would eat. I couldn't help but wonder how many such opportunities exist in Hardwick and, by extension, in other communities throughout our country.

"Baby food!" yelped Stearns, having been struck by yet another lightning-bolt idea. I dropped the piece of pumpkin in my hand

and looked up. He was so elated, I half expected him to levitate. "Organic baby food!" He squealed again, and started tossing pumpkin chunks with renewed fervor.

We gathered for about an hour, leaving Johnson's kitchen manager to finish filling the 20 or so bags he'd brought. When full, each weighed perhaps 60 pounds. It was a mere fraction of what lay on the ground, 1,200 or so of the half-million pounds High Mowing would generate over the coming weeks. But it was a start. As we left the field, I asked Stearns to describe the satisfaction he gets from envisioning and implementing this sort of venture. "Oh, it's huge," he said. "It's huge." That response didn't seem to satisfy the internal metric he applies to his answers, so after a brief pause, he continued speaking. "The potential we have and the time we have to do it is all lining up. Sometimes I feel like I'm overwhelmed by opportunity."

Stearns had invited me to the weekly employee potluck lunch at High Mowing, so I followed him down the hill to the company's offices and warehouse, which are situated in a long, low building along Route 15, about 4 miles west of Hardwick. There were two greenhouses located behind the building, and under a high, three-sided shed was an old combine used to harvest certain seeds. We parked and Stearns led me into one greenhouse where cucumber seeds were drying. The seeds had been spread across screens, and the room was full of window fans, 20 in total. "This is thousands of dollars of seed drying on window screen," Stearns told me. "It's a totally primitive design." He was clearly proud of the system's rudimentary nature.

We walked quickly through the greenhouse (once you've seen one cucumber seed, you've seen 'em all) and angled toward the room where High Mowing cleans and sorts seed. In one corner of the cement-floored room sat a pallet of dried cucumber seed in large bags, totaling about 225 pounds. At bulk, wholesale pricing, the seed was worth about $35 per pound, but after High Mowing broke it down into garden-market packets, it would gross nearly $700 per pound. Stearns could see that I was stunned by this disparity and quickly pointed out that High Mowing was on track to lose more than a quarter-million dollars for the year.

I was surprised by the austerity of High Mowing's seed-cleaning infrastructure. There were two machines in the room; one was a simple vertical metal spiral with a bucket at its base. The spiral was designed to separate seed from the chaff it picks up during its journey from field to market; mostly, this consists of small stones and plant stubble. It works best with round, uniformly sized seeds, which gather speed and gravitate to the outer edges of the spiral flutes while the impurities tumble through the center, to be discarded. From there, the seeds are transferred to a gravity table, which tilts in two directions while vibrating like a coin-operated bed in a cheap motel and blowing a strong current of air across the seed. The lower-density objects (seed, mostly) end up in one corner, while the higher-density objects (rocks that were missed by the spiral) end up in another. The seeds are now ready for packaging.

The whole system seemed wonderfully, seductively simple. And cheap: Stearns's total investment in seed-drying and seed-cleaning machinery came to less than $10,000. Of course, the greenhouses and cleaning room contained only a fraction of the process; it did not represent the cost of the farmland; the labor to sow, grow, and harvest the seed; the technical research into germination and yield; the Web site; the catalog; the marketing; the shipping; and so on. But I'd anticipated something grander, and I was glad to have been proven wrong. Growing, harvesting, and processing seeds, even for a commercial outfit like High Mowing, is still largely a human endeavor.

It was nearly noon, so Stearns and I strolled into the small lounge and kitchen area. A half-dozen or so High Mowing employees had gathered; there were a pot of corn chowder, a plate of thick-sliced bacon, two kinds of bread, a slab of cheddar cheese, and nine plates of melon, each of a different variety. Staff lunches at High Mowing also serve as informal taste tests. The walls were lined with books (*Climate and Man*, *Crops in Peace and War*, *Farmers in a Changing World*), recognitions (Lamoille County Farmer of the Year, the Social Responsibility Award from the Vermont Small Business Development Center), and little slips of paper on which employees had written short missives on what they most value about working for High Mowing (my favorite: "I like the fact that somewhere in some fancy chemical office some board of directors wishes we would go away"). A door along the back wall of the kitchen was open to the day; just beyond the opening sat a tall pile of kitchen scraps in the early stages of decomposition. I could have side-armed my melon rinds through the door and landed a direct hit to the compost pile, but I didn't, because this wasn't my home and I don't typically throw food when I've been invited to lunch. But I wanted to.

The Friday staff lunch at High Mowing is just one way the company fosters a communal atmosphere. It also maintains a line in its budget specifically for parties ("thousands of dollars," Stearns assured me) and provides its workers with as much free produce as they and their immediate family can eat. And because so many employees keep livestock or hunt, there's an annual "meat swap" where staff members can off-load extra chickens in exchange for a venison roast or two.

High Mowing employees do not receive health insurance, but they are given $2,000 each year to help defray medical expenses. Workers can spend the money at the health-care practitioner of their choosing. "They can get their chakras realigned for all I care," Stearns told me as we sat in the kitchen after his staff had returned to work. He grinned and lobbed a melon rind through the doorway. The salaries for management positions range from $33,000 to

$60,000, and hourly workers earn between $9 and $18 per hour. There's no quick road to riches at High Mowing, but in a town with a median income of under $15,000, these are enviable wages.

It's tempting to talk about High Mowing and the larger story of Hardwick in the soaring, metaphorical oratory of seed sowing, growth, and roots, all the more so because the company's founder is the man most associated with the town's local food movement. High Mowing produces the seeds to feed the town, to foster the local vegetable growers, to build the foundation of a healthy food system. This, in turn, provides the inspiration and maybe, someday, even the instruction to other communities. Seeds are being sown: seeds of knowledge, seeds of inspiration, and just plain seeds.

Tom Stearns himself is not afraid to help you draw these connections if he deems you're not drawing them yourself. He knows it has helped his company raise the money it needs to move into the realm of profitability (even in the rapidly deteriorating market conditions of mid-2008, he managed to cobble together $800,000 from a variety of socially responsible investors), and it has proved fertile ground for the media. How could it not? It's simple and evocative.

It's also not very fair to Tom Stearns and his employees. The long, hard slog of making High Mowing profitable while hewing to its core tenets of responsible growth and community betterment can't be summed up in a convenient metaphor. What of the stress, the late nights, the endless, looping emotional roller coaster of running a small business? Surely that's worth more than a pleasant, folksy allusion to growth and renewal.

After lunch, Stearns walked me to the door. I scurried through the warehouse trying to keep pace with the ever-ebullient seed baron as he trotted past pallets of seed packed into burlap bags, past the '50s-era machine that sorts the seed into packets, past a poster that read "We the indigenous puppeteers of the giant earth who is located in the sky in which she is also a midget" (I have no idea what the hell it means, either), past a row of prayer flags hung from the ceiling, past another poster proclaiming "God of the day: sky." I tried to reconcile what I'd seen that day—from the gleaning of waste squash in High Mowing's trial fields, to the communal employee lunch in the communal employee kitchen with its stone's-throw-distance compost pile, to this long, low building filled with enough organic, GMO-free seed to sprout thousands upon thousands of gardens and feed tens of thousands of people, to this fellow I followed, with his immense striving energy and vision—with what I was hearing from my friends in Walden. Steve and Suzanna had commented that Tom Stearns's version of agriculture wasn't a true alternative; that it had too much in common with the industrial, corporate model. Was everything I saw at High Mowing merely a stupid thing in a groovy ag movement? Was I simply too ignorant to understand their point? Because frankly, it seemed like one of the least stupid things I'd seen in a while.

Tom stopped short and, lost in thought, I almost bumped into him. "The thing is," he said, saucering his eyes, "no one else grows seed in Vermont, and there's a damn good reason."

This was apropos of nothing, or perhaps I'd missed the lead-in, but I nodded expectantly, waiting for the punch line.

"It snows eight months a year! I mean, how crazy do you have to be?" His laughter, a staccato trill, echoed through the warehouse.

CHAPTER TWELVE

A few days later, I again ventured to Hardwick for a fund-raising event being held at Claire's to benefit the Highfields Center for Composting. Bill McKibben had driven over from his Ripton, Vermont, home to lead a discussion of local food economies and then preside over a $65-per-plate dinner. I was pretty sure there was something ironic about the pairing of a local food and economy talk and a meal that cost the better part of a C-note in a town where the median income is under $15,000, but I couldn't quite put my finger on it.

I'd been making the drive to Hardwick frequently over the past few months, and I'd become enamored of how the road corkscrews its way into town. And I liked the view of Buffalo Mountain afforded by this stretch of pavement; to my way of thinking, it looked at once protective and welcoming. On warm days, I'd roll down the windows and let the air rush through the car as I leaned into the curves. But this day was not warm; a cool, soft rain was falling and the mountain was cloaked in a spectral mist. The weather matched my mood, which had been set by the news of the prior weeks. The US economy was in meltdown, and the airwaves were thick with dire predictions.

I arrived too late for the book discussion, but too early and too poor for the dinner, so I stopped in town and grabbed a couple slices of convenience-store pizza. In front of me in the checkout line were two 30-something men in work boots and blue jeans; the first purchased an enormous cup of black coffee and a handful of lottery tickets. The second bought a pack of Marlboros and a handful of lottery tickets. I paid for my pizza and then walked out into the rain, which was picking up. My mood was not improved. I briefly considered going back for a few lotto tickets.

For the next 45 minutes, I nibbled at my pizza (it was surprisingly good) and drove around Hardwick, nosing down every side street I could find and eventually climbing a long hill on its eastern edge that led to a circuitous loop through the rural landscape around town. I passed a restored Victorian painted a soothing deep green. I passed an old farmhouse. Cows grazed in the yard; one of them stood under a swing set, the chains of the swings laid over its wet flanks. At its highest point, the road changed from pavement to dirt and on either side, lush hayfields defined the topography. I imagined the scene in the winter, how the wind must whip across the fields, smearing snow and rattling the windows of the farmhouse.

It suddenly felt strange and wrong that I hadn't done this before; I'd been to Hardwick dozens, perhaps hundreds, of times during my adult life, but I'd never ventured beyond the main drag. I'd long had a sense of what the place was about, but it had been based almost entirely on the town's reputation and what I'd observed from my jaunts down Main Street. And what occurred to me now was not that'd I'd been wrong, but that I'd grossly underestimated the town's potential and the power inherent in that potential. The world economy was teetering. The centralized, industrial agriculture system, utterly dependent on that economy for its ongoing health, was facing mounting pressures. Hardwick certainly wasn't immune to the clouds drawing over our nation's economy. But because things had been tough for so long here, it didn't have as far to fall. There hadn't really been a boom in Hardwick, and therefore no one had splurged on the sort of easy credit that was beginning to collapse into a bankrupt heap. Its people already knew how to live with diminished expectations and resources. They'd done it for years; they could do it for a few more, and a few more after that. Would the town's food network be unaffected by a freeze in credit? Probably not. Would it be functional? Almost certainly.

By the time I pushed open the door at Claire's, my spirits had brightened considerably. Part of this sunny outlook rode on my hopes for Hardwick and for the lessons it might offer the wider world. But another part, I must confess, was less altruistic: It was immensely comforting to realize that I lived within the safety net of the town's food web. Maybe, if things got really bad, I'd lose my house. But I sure as hell wasn't gonna go hungry.

And some of it had to do with Claire's itself. The restaurant opened in late May 2008, with modest expectations for success. Hardwick has historically been a dive-bar-and-diner type of town; prior to Claire's, a handful of eateries had come and gone, none lasting more than a calendar year. The town's established restaurants—the Hardwick Village Diner, the Hardwick House of Pizza, and the Yummy Wok—make up a culinary landscape of fare served to a solid, working-class citizenry that rarely asks for more than solid, working-class food: meat loaf, burgers, french fries, calzones, and, when the occasion calls for something exotic, egg rolls and fried rice.

But there is something else that Claire's offers, something that seems to have taken root in part because it was planted and in part because the conditions for its growth were fertile: It provides a venue for people to come together, a place that's not work and not home, but something in-between. "The third place" is what writer and urban sociologist Ray Oldenburg calls it, a place that's separate from the first and second places of home and work but still connected to them. Third places are cornerstones of community life and facilitate the sort of social engagement essential to any healthy community. They are the places where ideas are born and debated, where groundswells arise in discussions over food and drink. It's telling that Starbucks has adopted the term in its marketing efforts, although I can only hope that people see that for what it is.

To be sure, Hardwick has other third places: the Village Diner is one, as is the Buffalo Mountain Food Co-op. For some, the liquor store seems to suffice. But the nature of Claire's, with its local food focus and, not to put too fine a point on it, bar, tends to cultivate a different level of engagement. People are encouraged to loiter for hours, and they do, gathered around the bar over pints of beer and glasses of wine or settled at a table in the dining room. Sometimes, it's both; Claire's is the sort of place where you can move from bar to table and back again, where you can drop in on a friend or acquaintance, where conversations often spread to neighboring tables. I know this because, under the guise of investigative reporting, I've been spending an awful lot of time at Claire's, particularly on Monday nights, when pints of local microbrews are $2.

The launch of Claire's had been a few years in the making; on a conceptual level, at least, it predated many of the food-based businesses that had garnered so much attention over the preceding months. But despite this, the opening of Claire's felt like confirmation of Hardwick's ag revival, and it wasn't hard to understand why. Here was a place that could tie it all together: steaks from Snug Hollow Farm, salad from Pete's Greens, cheese from Jasper Hill, eggs from Windhorse Farm, bread from Patchwork Bakery, and so on. It is true that many of Hardwick's 3,200 residents can't afford to eat at Claire's, where entrees run $12 to $24. But it is also true that the plates emerging from the small, open kitchen are symbolic of a functional local food system in an immensely appealing, visceral way. Maybe that's because it provided, in a very literal manner, an outlet for the region's producers. Or maybe it's because the food at Claire's simply tastes better and is more beautiful than what most of us prepare at home; it is like those spotless, perfectly decorated living rooms in a Pottery Barn catalog, both inspiring and, in the way something that we know is unattainable can be, somewhat dispiriting. But unlike, say, a leather sectional sofa, dinner at Claire's is inexpensive enough that we can come back again and again, perpetuating the illusion of ownership.

Actually, at Claire's, it's not really an illusion: The restaurant was founded on a unique ownership structure that included selling 50 "shares" to the public. For $1,000, anyone could buy a Claire's share, which entitled him or her to one $25 dinner credit per month until the investment was returned in full in the form of soups and steaks and pints of beer. Claire's calls itself a community supported restaurant (CSR), a riff on the community supported agriculture (CSA) model that is blossoming on small farms throughout the country. The basic idea is to have the consumer shoulder some of the risk while providing the producer with an infusion of cash at a critical juncture. On a farm, CSA shares are typically sold at the outset of the season, when the farmer is forced to lay out operating cash (seed, labor, fuel, and so on) without the benefit of having a crop to sell. A CSA share entitles the consumer to a weekly share of whatever the farm produces once the harvest comes in.

The CSR program at Claire's isn't the only thing that's unique about its operating structure. The restaurant was founded by four principals—chef Steven Obranovich, his domestic partner Mike Bosia, Kristina Michelsen, and Linda Ramsdell—who sublease the space and equipment from the Hardwick Restaurant Group, which was formed specifically to lower the barrier to entry for Claire's or, if the worst should come to pass and the restaurant fails, any future establishments. "The overarching goal is to provide the foundation and infrastructure for a restaurant business, any restaurant business, to succeed," Ramsdell explained. "This is something that Hardwick needs and wants, but it's not a particularly easy environment." Ramsdell, who owns the town's sole bookstore, is the only

Claire's owner who is also one of the ten private investors making up the Hardwick Restaurant Group, which assumed a 12-year lease on the building, paid for renovations, and bought the kitchen equipment. The group benefits by having equity shares in the restaurant, and the restaurant benefits by being nearly free of start-up debt.

Thus far, there seems to be little risk of failure. Six months after opening, in fall 2008, business was running 200 percent ahead of the group's most optimistic expectations. All summer, the place had been packed, churning out 100 to 150 dinners each night. Every time I stopped by, I couldn't help but notice that Obranovich, a tall, angular man with a penchant for rainbow-colored socks tucked into kitchen clogs, looked a little stunned. His hair stuck out in unlikely directions; behind a pair of wire-rim glasses his eyes were wide, as if each diner walking through the door was another pair of headlights bearing down on him in the dark. He'd hired the requisite assistants and dishwashers and such, but the kitchen was not ready to run without him, and he knew it. A few times, I approached him cautiously, hoping to talk, but I'd see his eyes widening even more as I drew near and I'd retreat to the bar to nurse a pint.

As surely as the success of Claire's was due to Obranovich's skill in the kitchen, it was also due to the restaurant's commitment to using local ingredients and the media frenzy that commitment drew. Obranovich had managed to source nearly 80 percent of his ingredients from within a 15-mile radius, and it was completely feasible for someone to order a dinner that had been assembled entirely from the Hardwick region. Booze is a sore spot; the closest brewery, Rock Art, is located some 30 miles to the west, in the town of Johnson. By the standards of Claire's, this is practically international trade. Too, most of the hard-alcohol standards are still taking the long road to their perch behind the bar. But in general, and especially by the time they'd found the bottoms of their second glasses, folks seem willing to excuse this particular glitch in the restaurant's supply chain.

I finally managed to corner Obranovich to make a date. I wanted to ask the sort of not-very-revealing-but-irresistible questions typically asked of chefs (Who were his influences? What was his favorite food? If he could eat only one thing for the rest of his life, what would it be? And so on), but I also wanted to understand his commitment to and interest in local foods. For instance, I'd heard from Kristina that Claire's would continue to serve dishes consisting of at least 70 percent local foods throughout the winter. To my ears, this sounded both overly ambitious and terribly lacking in variety. I imagined a menu comprised almost entirely of meat, cheese, and root crops that could handle long-term storage. Not such bad fare, in the scheme of things, but not the sort of stuff on which repeat business is built.

Obranovich finally admitted me on a Thursday. It was noon when I walked into Claire's, which opened for dinner at five o'clock. The restaurant's original plans had included a lunch seating, but the dinner business had proven so overwhelming that lunch was scuttled after only a month. In true community style, the restaurant's owners ran a large ad in the *Hardwick Gazette* explaining the decision and practically begging for forgiveness.

Obranovich had stepped out for a smoke, so I chatted with Kristina, who was wielding a plunger against the drain that serviced the bar. She looked as if she'd had plenty of practice; indeed, the clog soon surrendered with a satisfying "*glug*," and she raised the plunger in victory as Obranovich walked through the door.

I'd hoped to catch the chef at work in his kitchen, but Chef Obranovich seemed wary of admitting me into his workspace, particularly while he was actually working. Perhaps it had something to do with the size of the kitchen, which was maybe 8 by 16 feet and felt more than a bit claustrophobic, even without a bumbling journalist to navigate around. Or maybe he was simply concerned that I'd do something uncouth, like drop a pen into a tub of gravy or stumble and ignite my shirt on one of the 80,000-Btu burners of his industrial gas stove. Most likely, he just didn't want to be bothered; my impression was that he preferred to be left to his work and was not gladly suffering the hordes of reporters that had descended upon town in recent months.

So we sat at a table just outside the kitchen. On the wide shelf of the serving window between kitchen and dining room, a dozen quart canning jars were arranged in a neat row, filled with local blueberries and slightly less local vodka (it was from Maine). Next to the blueberry vodka were a few more jars, these filled with more vodka and vanilla beans. "Vanilla extract is just so expensive." Obranovich shook his head disapprovingly. "I figured it'd be cheaper to make my own." Beyond the jars of infused alcohol, trays of pale, spotted, and otherwise disadvantaged tomatoes, the last of the crop from Pete's Greens, were splayed across the kitchen counters. "I'm going to process all those without flavorings, so they're more versatile. I'm not sure what I'll do with them, but I'm not buying Florida tomatoes this winter, and I'll sure be glad to have these in January."

I should probably mention that to a certain extent, I'd discounted the restaurant's contributions to Hardwick's food system. On the face of it, this may seem absurd; after all, nearly every facet of the operation, from its unique ownership structure, to its unwavering commitment to local food, to the jobs it provided, to the vitality it had lent Hardwick's downtown, seemed emblematic of a functioning, nay, *vibrant* decentralized food system. But as obvious as all this seemed, Claire's still felt to me like—I'm not sure how else to put this—an extravagance not unlike, say, $20-per-pound cheese. Who wouldn't want to eat at Claire's? The food is excellent and the atmosphere is just classy enough to feel out of the ordinary and just low-key enough (there are no tablecloths and wine is served in jelly jars) that it feels appropriate to the town. No, the question isn't whether or not Claire's can stand on its own as an exemplar of everything it claims to be, but whether it's simply another example of a high-end product that only a handful of the town's residents can afford.

Okay, sure, not everyone in Hardwick wants to eat at Claire's, finances notwithstanding. They're missing out, no doubt about that, but at least that is their choice. But just as surely, there are folks in the region who might want to patronize the town's hip new restaurant, but simply can't. It's not that Claire's is overly expensive for the quality it offers. But even if prices are modest by the standards of the place, they put the food well out of reach for many locals. I know this because I feel it myself: I've eaten at Claire's a handful of times. Mostly, this was during my work for my *Gourmet* article, for which I had an expense account, and I'd simply ordered whatever was most expensive on a given night. But once, I treated Tom Stearns to dinner; the tab (which to be fair included a bottle of wine) came to $100. I thought about Ralph and Cindy Persons and how, to cover the meal Tom and I ate, they'd have to slaughter two pigs. I'm not sure if this is equitable or not, but somehow, it seems significant.

Obranovich is not oblivious to the issue of affordability and egalitarian access to his food. "I feel bad about it. I don't want to be perceived as precious and high-end. That's why we tried for a low-key atmosphere, no tablecloths, simple silverware. We want to cultivate a perception of accessibility." At the same time, he believes that Claire's, by dint of its relatively upscale décor and reputation as a new kid on the block with a backpack full of its local food mission, is perhaps being unfairly maligned for its prices. "Over at the diner"—he pointed across the street—"you've got entrées that cost $12. And here, you've got entrees that cost $12. Last time I checked, that's the same amount of money."

He makes a good point, and it's one that, without much stretching, can be applied to both Claire's and the broader local food movement. Is it possible that local food *isn't* actually more expensive than that which can be found along the aisles of the Grand Union? Forget about the externalities: the taxpayer subsidies, the sacrificed health, the environmental toll, and the depleted resources. I'm talking dollar in pocket for dollar in pocket.

To understand how this might be so requires considering the differences in how people cook with local ingredients compared to how they cook (or, to be more precise, don't cook) with processed foods. When you're shopping at a farmers' market or at the Buffalo Mountain Food Co-op, there is no TV dinner equivalent. There is no packaged, vitamin-and-mineral-enriched cold cereal hawked by cartoon characters or heat-and-serve frozen lasagna. These things might seem cheap when compared with restaurant food or when measured against the time it takes to actually cook something from scratch, but on a per-serving basis, they're not exactly frugal dining. In Hardwick, and in many other places around the globe, the raw ingredients of these meals can be procured from local sources for less than the processed versions cost.

Now, I have little doubt that one can eat inexpensively on a modern supermarket diet, assuming that one purchases the same basic ingredients that can be found at the farmers' market and puts the same amount of effort into turning them into nutritious meals. But based on my admittedly unscientific observations conducted while skulking about the aisles of Hardwick's Grand Union, I feel comfortable in saying that most don't. They partake of heavily processed, teasingly packaged, mostly prepared foods for any number of reasons: taste, convenience, advertising allure. And maybe, if they've even considered local foods as an alternative, because they *think* they're cheaper. When in fact, they are not.

This is all very anecdotal and by no means definitive. But that doesn't make it entirely wrong, either. The truth, as is so often the case, probably lurks somewhere in the middle. Local foods can be more expensive than supermarket foods or they can be less, a juxtaposition that exists because of the vast number of choices presented to us as consumers. The average American supermarket is stocked with nearly 50,000 products, and only a small fraction of these are raw ingredients. Still, as Obranovich so keenly points out, the damage might not be the facts, but the perception. And on this matter, there's little room for debate: Local food is almost unanimously *perceived* as being more expensive.

Which makes Obranovich's goal of ensuring the long-term success of Claire's all the more challenging. Hardwick is a small town with a proportionately small customer base. At some point, the buzz surrounding Claire's will fade; the novelty of traveling to Hardwick from Burlington (one hour) or Montpelier (35 minutes) to check out the cool new local food restaurant will fade. This phenomenon has been visited on almost every restaurant that has ever opened its doors, and Claire's will almost certainly be no different. Obranovich has worked in enough restaurants that he knows the score. "Unless we get all those people in Hardwick who haven't been in to come in, we won't make it," he told me matter-of-factly.

He doesn't mean this literally, of course; not even Tom Stearns possesses the irrational optimism necessary to believe that every one of the town's 3,200 residents will at some point walk through Obranovich's doors. What he means is that Claire's will have to succeed where the broader local food movement largely fails—by crossing socioeconomic boundaries to a degree that makes its business model viable. And, as circumstances would have it, by doing this during the sharpest economic downturn in eight decades.

Earlier, I noted that I'd largely discounted the contributions Claire's could make to the town's food system. But that was because, when I wrote that, I was thinking of food somewhat myopically, as something to be valued chiefly for its nutrients, flavor, and contribution to the human condition. These things are worth plenty, but Claire's, when seen in the light of the third place, adds an entirely different dimension, and does it in a way that's eminently more tangible than the sometimes amorphous claim of community rebuilding put forth by local food advocates. I know, because I've passed many long evenings in the place, too poor (or simply too cheap) to buy dinner, but still feeling nourished by a pint or two and conversations that move from the frivolous to the somber and back again, often in the span of a minute or less. I don't mean to offend Obranovich—he is a fine chef and his cooking is reason enough to visit Claire's—but I don't go for the food, and I wouldn't go for the food even if I could readily afford it. I go a little bit for the beer but mostly, I go for the people. This might not make the owners of Claire's any wealthier, but it sure makes me feel rich.

CHAPTER THIRTEEN

The town of Craftsbury, Vermont, isn't far from Hardwick; it takes maybe a dozen minutes to traverse the eight miles of pot-holed pavement that separates the two burgs, sluicing through a shallow valley rimmed by steep ridges just beyond the road's shoulder. To your right, at the end of a high gravel road that cuts a narrow path through the trees, sits Heartbeet Lifesharing, the residential farming community where my journey into Hardwick's evolving food system had begun. To your left, the forest is thick and foreboding and looks a likely place to become disoriented, run short of provisions and spend a frozen night fending off a pack of winter-starved wolves.

At least that's how it appeared to me in the low, late-afternoon light that filtered through an oppressive cloudbank as I made the drive to visit Pete Johnson. Johnson is the founder and proprietor of Pete's Greens, a mixed-vegetable and local food operation that runs the state's largest year-round community supported agriculture (CSA) program, with customers as far afield as Burlington, about an hour to the west. He calls his CSA "Good Eats"—a pleasingly folksy title that leaves me with a hankering for old-fashioned comfort foods like meat loaf and mashed potatoes, roast chicken and blueberry pie. Pete, I'm sure, would suggest rounding out the meal with a salad.

Like Tom Stearns and Andrew Meyer, Johnson has become inexorably linked to Hardwick's recent agriculture-derived fame. Indeed, he is friends with both Stearns and Meyer and sits on the board of the Center for an Agricultural Economy. He has, in a way that's quieter than that of his two buddies, aligned himself with the movement. He's also become something of a cover boy and media darling; it was his face that appeared on the front page of the *New York Times* Dining section, and in the summer of 2008, Johnson's smiling mug graced the cover of *Vermont Life* magazine. He is not blessed with the hyperkinetic social energy and nonstop inspirational banter of Stearns, and there's little of Andrew Meyer's beguiling, Opie-ish nature. Rather, Johnson's appeal seems to me largely centered on his tousled, devil-may-care good looks and his understated conversational manner. He isn't the type to make proclamations or otherwise draw attention to himself (though he's proven remarkably adept at promoting and growing his business), but when he speaks, his comments are thoughtful and precisely worded. And his attire, which rarely seems to vary from its field- and equipment-dirtied state, lends credibility to his words. The overarching impression is that here is a man who knows hard work and knows of which he speaks, and not because he's studied it in the abstract in a classroom (Middlebury College diploma notwithstanding) or delegated the laborious demands of his profession. I know this because I'd visited Johnson during the height of the autumnal harvest season; he was all but sprinting down the narrow aisles of dirt that separate lush beds of salad greens, harvesting the delicate leaves at a frenetic pace, utilizing a contraption of his own design. It looked like a fine-toothed saw blade attached to a bag because, well, that's pretty much what it was.

I was surprised to learn that Peter Johnson was born in Los Angeles; everything about his appearance and demeanor suggest a rural upbringing. Maybe that's because he didn't live in LA for long; when he was still a toddler, his parents, Richard and Nancy, moved to Oak Harbor, Washington, a small military town on Whidbey Island, with Pete and his older sister, Danica. There, they purchased five acres, built a small house, had two more children, and grew much of their own food. By age three, Pete worked in the family garden; by age six, he'd mentally designed a mechanical bean cultivator; by age nine, he had a booming pumpkin business. "My mom was raised in a traditional suburban household and then spent her adult life becoming more and more alternative," Pete told me. That alternative bent included packing up the four Johnson children and moving to Vermont when Pete was 12, because Nancy felt compelled to live in a four-season climate.

The Johnsons took to Vermont immediately; Pete became an avid skier, cyclist, and runner, and his younger brother Andrew is currently an elite-level cross-country ski racer. His sisters, Anners and Danica, live in the area and, like Pete, hold jobs involving soil and plants (Anners owns a small landscaping business; Danica runs a floral-design studio). In 2002, when Pete was 30, Nancy suffered a burst appendix and died in the Greensboro home that sits on the same land on which Pete launched his business. Richard still lives in the house; the greenhouse where Pete nursed his first seedlings to life still stands.

All of this is interesting enough, but what I found truly intriguing about Pete Johnson was the fact that, save a short stint as a carpenter following his college graduation, he has done nothing but grow vegetables. And he has only done so for himself; unlike many vegetable farmers, who get their fingernails dirty as an intern or field laborer at an established outfit, Johnson has learned practically everything he knows plying the time-tested method of trial and error. Pete's Greens began as a half-acre patch on his parents' land; eventually, he cleared another acre with a chain saw and hired an excavator to pull the stumps from the forest floor. As any experienced vegetable grower will tell you, this sort of toil—first the saw, then the brush clearing, then the cleanup from the machinery, then plowing the soil, then picking out the rocks and maybe plowing it again and picking out more rocks (in Vermont, there are always more rocks), then building soil fertility, and then, maybe, finally, sowing some sort of cover crop to loosen the earth with its tentacles of roots and feed it with its nitrogen—is like squeezing blood from a stone. But if you believe (and I do) that one measure of a person's passion is his willingness to dispense with excuses and make do with whatever lot he's been granted, then you won't doubt that Pete Johnson is pretty damn passionate about growing vegetables.

He has also benefited from being ideally positioned to capitalize on the wave of interest in local food. In 2004, he purchased a 230-acre swath of river bottomland on the outskirts of Craftsbury village, complete with an old, rambling dairy barn and a massive colonial where he now lives with his girlfriend, Meg Gardner. The 60 acres of tillable land on the property is exactly the sort of farmland vegetable growers find religion over: flat and stoneless, rich and well drained. Until the mid-'90s, it supported a small family dairy farm; more recently, it served as cropland.

The move was a boon to Johnson. For starters, it instantly increased his arable acreage by more than 400 percent (in addition to his original acre and a half, he had been leasing a 10-acre patch from a sheep farmer in the nearby village of Albany), allowing him to install half a dozen 200-foot-long greenhouses. And the infrastructure opened even more doors: He converted the bottom floor of the dairy barn into storage space and wash rooms, and he installed a large, industrial kitchen in the farmhouse (the one with the "big-ass" kettle and the pulper that smashed the "bejesus" out of things) so that he might take advantage of opportunities as they availed themselves, such as the squash from High Mowing's fields. He split the rest of the house into two apartments, enabling him to provide housing for the family of Mexican field laborers that has spent the past four summers on the farm.

There is also an office, and that's where I found Johnson when I arrived. Truthfully, "office" is a generous word for the space, which is basically a large, empty (and on this winter day, very cold) room with a desk and a computer pushed against one wall. Predict-ably, Johnson, who is lean and short but somehow never appears insubstantial, was clad in work clothing: faded sweatshirt and car-penter jeans. He'd kicked off his rubber barn boots, revealing a pair of white cotton socks which were probably the cleanest article of clothing I'd ever seen him wear. I remembered running into John-son and Gardner one summer evening at Claire's, when they were out for dinner. Meg had been wearing a stylish black dress and hoop earrings; Pete was sporting a sweater and work pants and looked as if he might have just emerged from under a tractor.

I plopped into a chair and maneuvered myself as close to the insufficient wall-mounted heater as possible, but before I could profit from its meager flame, Johnson was called to the kitchen by one of his workers to assess a 40-gallon batch of chicken broth that had been simmering for the past four hours. This was exactly the sort of opportunity Johnson had imagined when he installed the kitchen. He'd procured for less than a dollar per pound a steady supply of local, free-range chicken carcasses, which he dumped into the pot 80 pounds at a time, along with cosmetically chal-lenged carrots and onions from his fields and a whole bunch of water. The total cost to him, he figured, was about $1.50 per quart. And the retail value? Perhaps four times that.

"I don't do a lot of thinking about what's coming, about what I'm going to do next," he told me as he jammed a screwdriver handle-deep into the kettle's flow valve, which had clogged with broth detritus. "It's more just responding to opportunity, and being positioned to take advantage of that opportunity." To wit: a bubbling cauldron of chicken broth consisting of local ingredients and destined for the soup pots of the participants in Johnson's Good Eats CSA program.

Good Eats is built on roughly four-month cycles; each 17- or 18-week period costs $748 and includes a weekly basket of seasonal vegetables and a few additional treats from local producers. For the month of November 2008, a weekly share looked something like this:

2 festival winter squash

¾ pound winter greens

1 bunch kale

2 pounds Ailsa Craig onions

2 pounds carrots

1 pound pak choi

2 pounds Yukon gold potatoes

1 napa cabbage

5 pounds rolled oats

1 dozen eggs

½ pound Jasper Hill clothbound cheddar

All the vegetables were grown on Pete's farm; the oats were from Quebec; the eggs were from a farm down the road; and the cheese was from the Cellars at Jasper Hill, a few miles up the road in Greensboro. If things went well, Good Eats members would soon be the recipients of the chicken broth I'd seen in Johnson's kitchen. The shares would be distributed to each of Johnson's 250 CSA members, via coordinated drop-off points in Vermont population centers. Johnson doesn't have a firm geographical boundary for his CSA, although he recently turned down an opportunity to enter the Boston market. Still, critics might argue that with less than 10 percent of its CSA clientele coming from the immediate region (at the time of my visit, there were 24 customers in the Craftsbury-Hardwick region), Pete's Greens isn't really doing much to feed the locals, and that driving CSA shares an hour west to Burlington is questionable practice for a business trading on the word "local."

Indeed, for reasons that took me a while to decipher, Pete Johnson has become something of a target for criticism. Some of it is surely his definition of "local," which he seems inclined to extend to Vermont's southern border with Massachusetts, some 150 miles distant. A portion of it can probably be pinned on his youth and ambition; farming, even organic vegetable farming, is a craft imbued with culture, tradition, and unspoken rules of conduct. Into this comes Pete Johnson, with all his talk about movable greenhouses and four-season growing and community supported agriculture and, well, you can almost see the old-timers shaking their heads at the impudence of youth. And then people start to listen to him and his business grows so fast he can barely keep up, and all of a sudden Pete Johnson is the one appearing on magazine covers and being asked to give presentations. The young upstart tripping over the toes of the old sages: It's the oldest damn story in the book.

Another part of it—indeed, the part I found most intriguing— was the scale on which he operates: In the context of organic vegetable farming in a state of 600,000, having 60 acres of tillable land, 30 of which might be in production at any particular time, puts him in a lonely league. "There's no question that Pete's breaking from the model of organic vegetable farming that was formed in the '70s," Jessie Schmidt told me. Schmidt is the manager of the Montpelier farmers' market, a vibrant, weekly affair only two blocks down the street from the state capitol building. Pete's Greens is one of the largest—if not *the* largest—vendors at the market. Schmidt said, "I think there's always been this assumption that this sort of farm should be small enough for a family to run, and should only sell direct to market." (Johnson does a rousing wholesale business to co-ops and restaurants.) "So here comes Pete, he's young, he's ambitious, he's running a big operation, and he's not going to apologize for doing things differently. Some people are put off by that. But I think a lot of it's based on assumptions rather than facts."

Johnson certainly is ambitious; there's no question about that. Shortly after I arrived, we walked down a curving, quarter-mile farm road to the place where he recently constructed an equipment storage and maintenance building. Inside, sitting on wooden blocks with its wheels removed, was a specialized cultivating tractor he'd sent his maintenance man to Alabama to retrieve. Now, Johnson was tearing the tractor down to its bare frame for restoration. We pushed open a door just past the tractor (or what remained of it) and entered a small, warm room that carried the moist smell of plant growth. The room was full of sprouts, mostly sunflower, but some daikon and alfalfa. "I've always wanted to try sprouts," he told me. "They're such cool plants, so explosive in growth. It's crazy." He leaned over and put his face inches above a particularly verdant tray, softly stroking it with his left hand, as if he were petting a dog. Like the chicken broth now cooling in his farm kitchen, these sprouts were destined for Good Eats, although he wasn't ruling out the possibility of expanding the sprout operation to his wholesale markets.

And he's not the least bit apologetic regarding the scale of his operation, which he views as a complement to, rather than a competitor of, the region's multitude of smaller outfits. "Because of our size, because of our outlets, we're making it really easy for other local producers to get stuff to market," he says. "We're like this force that's creating more local products." He again petted the sprouts. "I just don't see what the downside is."

The issue of scale is one that permeates virtually every facet of Hardwick's food movement and should permeate every facet of every food system anywhere. Surprisingly, it's an issue that's been largely absent from the national discussion regarding local (and decidedly nonlocal) foods, and I'm pretty sure I know why: It might be an impossible question to answer. You could ask a hundred different people what constitutes an appropriate scale, and you'd probably get 500 answers, because each person would change his or her mind at least five times. They'd probably all agree that it's dependent on a multitude of factors, but exactly what those factors are and how much weight each should carry are considerations that come bookended by shifting sands.

To the extent that a discussion about food systems can achieve wonkishness, the following paragraphs probably do just that. But it's an important issue. Scale, and more specifically, appropriate scale, might be as critical to the local food discussion as simple geography is. After all, anything and everything is local to somewhere; a 1,000-acre soybean field outside Ames, Iowa, and the sprawling tomato fields in Homestead, Florida, are both geographically fixed near and within population centers. They are, arguably, local to those population centers. Now, they may not feed any of those locals; in fact, they probably don't, unless the complex and circuitous route of a soybean destined to become filler in some processed foodstuff or another by fate or coincidence ends up in the frozen foods case at a Safeway in Ames. The absurdity of our national food system might very well see those Homestead, Florida, tomatoes shipped to New York City, while the supermarkets in Homestead stock their produce aisle with California's best. But by the most base, unexamined definition of the word, those soybeans and tomatoes are local to someone, and by dint of this fact, they provide an opportunity to abuse the term.

What is the appropriate scale for agriculture? Notice I didn't ask "What is the appropriate scale for *local* agriculture?" because if we address the issue of appropriate scale, we inherently address the issue of geographical domain, with one exception: the importing of fertility, which is its own vexation, particularly for someone attempting to establish agriculture in a region that lacks the essential underpinnings. To understand all this, consider: An operation that's too big for its locality will find itself needing to exploit other, more distant markets in order to off-load its product. And in doing so, it will compete with operations in these markets, forcing them to lower their prices and then extend *their* reach in order to survive. It becomes a race to the bottom.

Meanwhile, an operation that's too small for its locality might struggle with economies of scale, which could force it to charge more than its customers can afford. This, in turn, will ensure only that its product remains the providence of the affluent or, alternatively, will simply drive the producer out of business. In theory, an operation of an appropriate scale will benefit from certain economies and efficiencies of that scale, helping to pull prices lower without eroding profit or denying other producers access to the market. Meanwhile, that same appropriateness of scale disallows supply-chain agriculture.

Earlier, I said it might be an impossible question to answer, and that might be true. It doesn't mean we shouldn't try. We can begin with the extremes. For instance, we know that the scale we're operating on now doesn't work. The fertilizer, the transport, the vulnerability; we've been through the issues time and time again, so I won't go into exhaustive detail here. If you've read this far, I'll assume that we're of a like mind regarding the outsize industrial food chain. Indeed, there would be little reason to have this discussion if we all felt that the current scale was healthy, sustainable, and something on which we should hang our future.

On one extreme, therefore, we have the status quo: the storied 1,500-mile iceberg lettuce, the 1,000-acre soybean farm, the tractor-trailer loads of green tomatoes (tomatoes are shipped green and hard to reduce transport damage, then exposed to the hydrocarbon gas ethylene to induce ripening) rumbling up Interstate 95, the single food calorie that soaked up 11 fossil-fuel calories on its journey from seed to plate. These are all examples of scale run amuck, of size and scope being determined strictly by economic metrics in a world where those metrics are based on some very naive and shortsighted calculations.

At the other extreme, we have, well, me. I've already mentioned that my wife and I don't even calculate the fiscal return on the agricultural labors at our little farm, in part because there's not enough return to justify calculating. The other part of our "by-the-seat-of-our pants" approach is that we don't really care how much money our farm brings in; we do this because we have come to understand that the value of the food we grow isn't the food minus the labor necessary to bring it to the table. It is the food *plus* the labor. I can buy a fine potato from any number of local farmers, including Pete Johnson, but I can't buy the May afternoon I spent with Penny in the garden, sticking our hands deep into the cool soil. I can buy a head of lettuce, but I can't buy the pleasure and pride of my two boys returning from the garden with a basket of greens and saying, "We picked it ourselves, Papa."

Still, the question isn't how much we love playing in the dirt, but whether, in the context of the 21st-century American economy, our enterprise is viable. Under such scrutiny, I must acknowledge that it's not of a scale that makes much sense for anyone who doesn't actually enjoy driving fence posts and popping potato beetles. Is it local? Hell, yes. Is it profitable? Hell, no.

The scale on which my family and I grow food is arguably inefficient, in terms of economics, efficiency, and land use. We don't utilize chemical fertilizers, synthetic weed and pest controls, or genetically modified seed; these things could probably boost our production in the short run, but then, we don't farm for the short run. We choose to eat meat for reasons of health, a deep and abiding belief in the restorative power of bacon, and farm synergy, because a farm without animals is a farm that must import significant quantities of fertilizer. Our animals don't merely feed us; they feed the soil. We maintain a towering stack of composting manure, bedding, waste hay, and vegetable scraps, and we spend hours every late April slinging spadefuls onto our gardens and around our fruit trees. Our farm is diverse to the point of absurdity. Last year, we raised, in no particular order: beets, potatoes, corn, squash (acorn, butternut, sunshine), green beans, peas, garlic, blueberries, strawberries, raspberries, lettuce, spinach, eggs, chickens (see? The egg does come first), cattle, tomatoes, green and red bell peppers, cabbage (all of which we turned into sauerkraut), pigs, ducks, lambs, maple syrup, celeriac, apples, gooseberries, turnips, kale, parsnips, and milk and all its sibling products (butter, yogurt, cheese, and, most especially, ice cream). There was more, but you get the idea.

But as much as we might value our kaleidoscopic gardens and our menagerie of beast and fowl, it is far more efficient to grow two acres of lettuce than two acres of mixed vegetables, with all their varying nutritive, land use, and tending demands. Too, our land is not ideal for growing food; it is hilly, and although the soils are fertile and well drained, they're peppered with stones. We have three gardens, not so much because we want three gardens, but because there's simply not enough cohesive flatness to support a single plot. In many ways, it's not unlike that small patch of bony cropland that Pete Johnson coaxed from the forest in Greensboro.

The point is not that we should stop doing what we do; it is merely to illustrate the other end of the spectrum, where the scale has become so diminished there is little efficiency or economic justification to it. I've never really tried to put a dollar figure on our harvest; it's been so long since we purchased a significant portion of our food that I've lost all context. And we eat so differently from most Americans that it's not realistic to use readily available figures to calculate our food budget. But I don't doubt that we raise $10,000 worth of food in a calendar year and that our input costs (seed, fertility, equipment) are significantly less than that.

That's all well and good, until I consider the endless hours invested. There's no time clock at Hewitt Acres; we don't punch in and out every time we enter the garden to pull a few weeds or head out to the barn to hurl a bale of hay at the cows. But we surely average at least 30 hours per week between the two of us, and probably much more. In the summer, it might be 50; in the winter, it might be 10. Fifteen hundred hours per year, for $10,000. No health care, no sick time, no paid vacations. If our nation were one of subsistence farms (I suppose ours would fall under this imprecise heading), it stands to reason that the broader economy would be structured in a way that did not resign the owners of these holdings to abject poverty. As it is, however, our farm doesn't generate enough economic activity to provide a reasonable income; it is not of a scale that allows us to carve a living from it. From a financial standpoint, we'd be far better off pursuing other careers and leaving the growing to someone else. Like Pete Johnson, for instance.

Or perhaps Eliot Coleman. Coleman lives in Harborside, Maine, near the infamous homestead of Helen and Scott Nearing, whose 1954 book *Living the Good Life* spawned the modern back-to-the-land movement (insomuch as the back-to-the-land movement can be described as "modern"). Coleman and his wife, Barbara Damrosch, preside over a mixed-vegetable and flower operation called Four Season Farm. They have quietly emerged as American pioneers in the business of small-scale, intensive, and—here's the kicker—profitable vegetable farming, having collectively written seven books and having spent the past four decades honing their operation. Coleman has created a cottage industry with his customized gardening tools, which are simple, human-powered contraptions often inspired by implements he's seen and used during his extensive travels in the agrarian regions of Europe. He has also designed and lent his name to a line of movable greenhouses; in the organic gardening community, Coleman is known for his ability to cultivate greens long into the harsh Maine winters without supplemental heat.

Coleman's done a lot of thinking about scale, and he has basically devoted his life to proving that small-scale operations can fill
both plates and wallets. "I happen to be a big fan of small," he told
me when I called him early one January morning. "It's important
for democracy to have a certain percentage of people feeding themselves so they can tell the government to go fuck off." I'd long ago
learned that there's a bit of revolutionary lurking in every small-
scale farmer; in this regard, Coleman is no exception to the rule.

But in another regard, he is. In 2008, Four Season Farm
grossed $120,000 from an acre and a half, providing Coleman and
Damrosch with an eminently livable wage off a piece of land that's
not much bigger than many suburban house lots. Indeed, he probably earned more money on his acre and a half than many Nebraska
corn farmers earn on 1,000 acres of premium breadbasket topsoil.
Still, Coleman's success is built on decades of research, experimentation, and backbreaking toil. "Nobody gets into this game because
they want to make money," Coleman says. "They get into it because
they have a sickness." I waited for him to laugh, but he didn't.

Too, despite the diminutive size of his farm and his professed
preference for small, he holds a dim view of those who might complain that an operation like Pete's Greens is too big. "Yes, my personal preference is to have a greater number of small, competent
producers, but how many people are competent to do what Pete is
doing? I've been around a while; I've seen a lot of incompetent
farmers go under. That's not exactly helpful, is it?" He was getting
a little worked up. "Look, the tendency toward bigger farms, with
more of the successful guys buying out the smaller guys, was going
on in horse-farming days. I don't think that's about to change."

He's equally unapologetic regarding the price premium that
goes with local, low-input food. "I'm working 60 hours a week,
thank you very much. If you choose not to get off your ass and do
this . . . " He trailed off, then slipped back into revolutionary mode.

"I think small farmers are the last bastion protecting society from corporate industry. When we feed ourselves, we become unconquerable." I thought of Tom Gilbert and his views on compost as a protagonist of community sovereignty.

My conversation with Coleman gave me plenty to mull over. Mostly, it made me question my career choice and farming skills. A hundred and twenty grand on an acre and a half? Good lord. What the hell am I doing writing a book? But it also made me realize that there is another factor that might help define appropriate scale: appropriate skill. Pete Johnson's operation has become what it is—both in terms of size and profitability—in no small part because Pete Johnson is damn good at what he does. A food system is only as viable as its ability to deliver food, come torrential rain, insufferable drought, or locust plague. Maneuvering a farm through the vagaries of nature demands a high degree of skill, and that it is precisely the skill that lends farmers like Pete Johnson and Eliot Coleman a significant competitive advantage. Would Hardwick's food system be healthier and more secure if there were 20 highly skilled farmers each tending an acre and a half, rather than one Pete Johnson tending 30 acres? Well, yeah, it probably would. Are there 20 farmers with the skills and the desire to, as Coleman so delicately put it, get off their asses? That is an entirely different question.

I was less convinced by Coleman's price argument; I don't believe it's merely laziness that stands between the blue-collar working class and locally produced food. I believe it's much deeper than that. In part, it is the result of misplaced priorities and externalized expenses that make it all but impossible to assign a true cost to our industrialized diet. On a more tangible level, it is simple access to land. Until our priorities shift so profoundly that we're willing to reconsider the model of property ownership that has prevailed in this country since settlement days, land access will remain the chief impediment to self-sufficiency in terms of food. For the time being, at least, we must grapple with the issue of local food access not through the lens of individual production (which should remain part of the conversation and solution), but through the lens of price.

It's possible to consider ways in which that might change. When our long-distance industrial food system reaches the breaking point, we might begin to value food on a level that's almost impossible to imagine now. If and when we return to an economy in which we're again devoting nearly a third of our income to feeding ourselves, for whatever reason, then perhaps the lower range of appropriate scale will drop to include our little farmlet (meanwhile, Eliot Coleman and Pete Johnson will be wheeling around on brand-new John Deeres and smoking Cuban cigars as they tend their plots). Or maybe our competence as farmers will evolve to the point where, like Eliot Coleman, we can secure a living off an acre and a half of mixed vegetables. But for now, for better or worse, we have the economy and skills we have, and our little agricultural enterprise remains primarily a labor of love, vibrant in spite of, not because of, any real economic rationale.

Of course, given the yawning chasm that separates our farm and the global food conglomerates that dominate the supermarket aisles, these examples don't exactly establish the framework necessary to reach any definitive conclusions regarding scale. However, they do illustrate two important truths: A food system based solely on economics and efficiency doesn't build community or security. In fact, it undermines these resources. Okay, big surprise, we knew that. What's more intriguing to me is to consider the other end of the spectrum: How much, exactly, does a system committed to community betterment and food sovereignty need to take on the characteristics of companies based on economics and efficiency of scale in order to participate in the broader US economy and provide the financial recompense necessary to cultivate not just a healthy crop, but a new generation of farmers?

There are obvious factors that might dictate the answer to such a question and they are, in no particular order: What sort of population and demand is the producer attempting to satisfy? Clearly, the appropriate scale for a farm serving Hardwick, Vermont, is going to be very different from the appropriate scale for a farm serving Chicago. What does the land resource base look like? Are there numerous opportunities for numerous producers to work together in a synergistic fashion, or is the productive ag land centralized and unique to the region? Is the community full of willing (and, no less important, capable) farmers, or is there another industry that adequately provides for the locals, making them reluctant to take up shovel and hoe? Lack of interest in the profession could certainly be seen as an argument for larger-scale operations run by the few folks possessing the will and the way.

Living within a stone's throw of Hardwick, with its tremendous bounty of arable land and engaged, passionate food producers, it's easy to forget just how good I have it, how good everyone in this quiet little community has it. In Hardwick, no one pulls back the curtains to see the cracked earth of relentless drought or a sweep of oil-stained asphalt. This is a community steeped in agrarian values and skills, and it plies those values and skills on an endowment of fertile soil. We have the luxury of debating the finer points of scale, of turning up our collective nose at the notion of importing fertilizer, of even asking the questions I've asked in the preceding paragraphs. We can debate things like whether or not Pete Johnson's 30 acres of organic vegetables and 40-gallon batches of chicken broth are of an appropriate scale. In so many other towns across the United States—indeed, in the majority of towns across the United States—where the choices are limited to Price Chopper and Safeway, Pete Johnson would be an unassailable agent

of positive change. Even in the context of Hardwick's good agricultural fortune, to most, he still is. It's important to note that the
criticisms of Pete's Greens, like the criticisms of Hardwick's agre-
preneureal movement as a whole, come from a small but vocal
minority.

I realize that I've just written a lot about appropriate scale and
not reached any coherent conclusions. As I warned, there are no
easy answers. Appropriate scale is a fluid term that must be adjusted
to account for a multitude of factors: population, resources both
physical and intellectual, industry, will, economy. And, I'd argue,
it has been so long since we've operated our food system on the
basis of appropriate scale—indeed, it's been so long since we've
even *thought* about appropriate scale—that we don't really know
how to have the conversation. We've spent the past century wor-
shipping at the altar of Bigger. Many of us have decided to back
away; a few, perhaps, have decided *how* to back away. But where do
we stop backing away? Where does Too Big meet Too Small to
become Just Right? We have much work to do before that question
can be definitively answered.

For his part, Pete Johnson isn't making any claims regarding
the appropriateness—or lack thereof—of his farm. He finds real
benefits in his larger scale, but he notes the challenge he's faced in
finding good workers and how vulnerable he is to the labor market.
"There's a real lack of security from not knowing if someone's
going to show up for work," he told me. "There was a certain point
where that suddenly became a really important and scary part of
my life. Maybe that's an argument that we're too big."

If so, it's not slowing him down much. Only a few years after
increasing his cultivated acreage fourfold, Johnson is looking for
more land, buying a bigger tractor, and thinking about ways to get
more of his food into the market. But he seems to recognize the
stigma attached to growth within the local food movement and

that perhaps it is best for a person of his ambition and ability to keep his head down and his hands in the dirt, even as his thoughts run toward expansion. "Tom Stearns will say, 'I want to start a 10,000-member CSA and I want to do it with you,'" Johnson told me. "And I say, 'Tom, that thought wanders through my head, too, but whatever you do, don't talk about it.'" Then, perhaps realizing that he'd revealed a bit too much: "Aren't these sprouts amazing?"

About a week after I visited Pete Johnson, and only a few days after I wrote everything you just read, I happened to share a car ride with the Toms. We were driving to Burlington for a meeting to discuss the recently formed partnership between the University of Vermont and the Center for an Agricultural Economy. And we were talking about scale.

I asked each for his definition of "appropriate scale"; predictably, each had plenty to say. Gilbert proceeded in a confessional tone. "I know that Highfields has cut into the local farmers' compost sales," he said. We were driving the same road I'd driven with Ralph and Cindy Persons a few weeks before, and I couldn't help thinking about the different tenors of the conversations on these two days, and how they could be so completely different and yet so completely relevant. "I know it and I feel bad about it. But I also know that in order to provide the services we want to provide and that this community needs, we need to grow. Does that make it wrong?" There was a pause; I waited for him to answer his own question, but he didn't.

Tom Stearns waited a beat or two; I could actually feel him waiting, his presence has such coiled exuberance. This was the first time I'd seen him in a few weeks, and he'd grown a bushy, red-tinged beard that had an effect opposite to the one expected of facial hair: It made him look as if he were trying to look older, which of course made him appear younger. "Maybe the question isn't 'How do you know when the scale is appropriate,' but 'How do you know when it's not appropriate?'" He was leaning forward in his seat, an eager puppy. "There's this assumption that big is bad, but maybe it's just that big is only bad when it's doing bad things." He started into another sentence, but Tom Gilbert had roused himself from the reverie that had followed his unanswered question.

"None of us has it right." It was clear, somehow, that he wasn't talking merely of the issue of scale, or even about food systems. He was talking about each of us, as members of this community, fallible and fraught with contradiction and assumptions. "We've all got it so wrong that we can't afford to think we've got it right."

At which point, something extraordinary happened: Tom Stearns shut up.

CHAPTER FOURTEEN

As I've already mentioned, Hardwick's food infrastructure did not begin where this tale commenced, with Tom Stearns pontificating on the woes of industrial ag and pitching his vision of how the town could become a beacon of healthy agriculture. It didn't begin with the launch of High Mowing Organic Seeds, Vermont Soy, Pete's Greens, the Center for an Agricultural Economy, Claire's Restaurant, the Highfields Center for Composting, or any of the businesses that have garnered so much recent attention. It didn't begin with the first pig Ralph and Cindy Persons slaughtered; it didn't begin the first time Forrest Foster knelt beside a cow to attach the tentacles of his milking machine to her milk-swollen udder. It didn't start the day the Buffalo Mountain Food Co-op opened its doors to the public.

Of course, all of these things happened, and all have played a role in making Hardwick what it is and what it will become. And at some point, as the rest of America chased its food farther up the corporate ladder, Hardwick became first a deviation from the norm and then a collective identity. It's not just the food that defines this identity; it's a sort of rural pride and aptitude for surviving and even thriving in the often-harsh landscape of back-road America. To live in Hardwick demands a level of responsibility for oneself and one's neighbor that's largely absent from modern, first-world life. Responsibility to cut the firewood not just when it's convenient, but in June, when the blackflies are as thick as saw oil, so it will season properly for the upcoming winter. Responsibility to know which water lines in the old farmhouse are most prone to freezing and to remember to wrap them in a little insulation or maybe an old T-shirt when the mercury in the thermometer drops below zero. Responsibility to know who in the neighborhood might have fallen on hard times and to know that a gift of firewood or half a frozen hog or even plowing their driveway after a snowstorm is a gift as good as cash. Maybe even better.

At first blush, it might seem as if none of this has much to do with decentralized food, but of course it has everything to do with it. To engage in a local food system is to assume a level of responsibility for the very thing that keeps you alive. If you're a producer, you assume that responsibility for yourself and your customers. If you're a merchant, you assume the responsibility of connecting farmer and consumer and of ensuring that each walks away from the transaction the better for it. If you're a consumer, your primary responsibility isn't to yourself, but to the people who keep your sustenance trickling down its truncated supply chain. Which, conveniently enough, only ensures your continued survival.

This is the sort of interconnectedness that once defined every outpost across our emerging nation. But outposts grew into towns, towns grew into cities, and cities grew into metropolises, necessitating a push into resource bases far beyond these population centers. Even as this occurred, the conveniences of modern life—electricity, indoor plumbing, the automobile—took hold, further eroding any sense of shared responsibility for the community's survival. From the standpoint of our most basic needs, we became islands unto ourselves, despite ever-increasing population density.

Of course, this happened in Hardwick, too; it just happened less. Part of it was the rural, closed-off nature of the place, but I think the visceral, life-and-death realities of the granite industry had something to do with it, too. The largest of the stone blocks weighed 60,000 pounds; in 1897, train tracks were laid between the main quarry and the stone sheds, but prior to this, the stones were transported by horse and wagon. It took as many as 40 draft animals to pull these loads, 20 rows of paired beasts, all muscle, lung, and obstinacy. The tremendous weight of these long trains of creature and stone frequently crushed the culverts crossing beneath the wagon track. Consider for a moment the level of communication and trust moving such massive pieces of rock demanded, particularly given the steam-driven, cable-winch technology of the day.

The ethic of interconnectedness became even more entrenched during the region's dairy-farming era, for the farming technology of the early 1900s wasn't what it is today. Now, using a round baler driven by a 100-plus-horsepower tractor, a single farmer can put up a month's worth of feed in a day. He rolls the hay into enormous, 1,000-pound marshmallows and stacks it with a clamping, grapple attachment connected to the tractor's front loader, or by spearing it with an ominous-looking shaft of steel. It's entirely possible that, in the 21st century, a farmer might put up a season's worth of hay without actually touching the stuff with his hands. I'm making this all sound far easier than it is, but the point remains: Modern dairy farming, even on a relatively small scale, replaces human labor with fossil-fuel-powered technology.

But the modern round baler wasn't invented until 1972; prior to that, putting up hay was a "many hands make light work" sort of task. It took one set of hands to drive the tractor and then, when the 50-pound square bales (they're actually rectangular, but "square" is easier to say, so that's what they're called) dotted the field like a bad back waiting to happen, at least another two pairs to throw and stack them, perhaps 200 to a wagon. Then the wagon had to be pulled to the barn, where the whole process had to be undone: The bales unloaded, stacked tight, and then, slowly, over the course of many snow-driven months, cut open and scattered at the mouths of hungry livestock. If rain threatened, reinforcements were called in. (One of the major advantages of round bales is that even if the hay gets wet, the bales can be wrapped and allowed to ferment. If square-bale hay gets rained on, it's ruined.) This is why, only a half-century ago, farming was a much more communal occupation than it is today. It was not uncommon for a group of farmers to simply move as a squadron from one farm to the next over a three- or four-week period, trying to get everyone's hay into the barn without its being sacrificed to rain.

In any event, I believe it was, in large part, Hardwick's ethic of interconnectedness that drew '70s-era back-to-the-landers to town as if they were winter-starved bees and it was a pot of spring honey. I think they had a desire to take responsibility, to insert themselves into a community and a landscape that had been built on interdependence. It's no original thinking on my part to note that this period in US history was one of disillusionment and confusion. In many, many ways, it was a decade of coming apart. Hardwick offered an opportunity to return to a way of life that felt rooted in soil and something equally substantial: humanity. It offered an opportunity to come together around a set of values that were sadly absent from the American way of life.

At least, that's how Louie Pulver and Annie Gaillard saw it. Louie and Annie live in Walden, a couple of miles down a hard-packed dirt road from my friends Steve and Suzanna. They've lived there since 1983, in a simple-but-fetching cedar-shingled house they built themselves. The window trim is painted bright purple; a barn beside the house provides shelter for the couple's three horses and sports a large peace sign. They operate a five-acre mixed-vegetable farm called Surfing Veggies, so named for Louie's affinity for longboards and ocean waves. The farm is certified organic; when Annie and Louie received their certification, there were 17 certified organic farms in Vermont. Now, there are nearly 600.

To further the dubious connection between surfing and vegetable farming, Louis trucks his surfboard to the Hardwick farmers' market, sets it atop a pair of sawhorses, and spreads his wares across its top. When I visited him and Annie shortly after the New Year, I entered through a small, cluttered room that contained a large box of carrots, two snowboards, and half a blueberry pie. Just outside the front door, a long row of garden implements hung against the wall: hoes, forks, spades, and rakes. The house is solar powered; a small array of photovoltaic panels was angled to greet the winter sun. To say the place felt like a cliché would be unkind, but not unjustified. If I'd tried to imagine exactly what a homestead belonging to one of Hardwick's original back-to-the-land couples would look like, I couldn't have done much better than to imagine precisely what I saw.

I sought out Annie and Louie for two reasons. One, they embody the agrarian back-to-the-land movement that laid the foundation for the current Hardwick-area ag revolution, and two, their immersion in the town and its food scene has been nothing less than total. In addition to her vegetable-tending duties at Surfing Veggie, Annie has worked at the Buffalo Mountain Food Co-op almost since its inception, when it was located on Portland Street and shared a building with a gun shop and a liquor store. It's possible that at some point in the history of the United States, there has been a place where, under one roof, you could purchase a pistol, a pint of Jim Beam, and a pound of tofu, but it seems more possible that there hasn't. The fact that such a building existed in Hardwick is as illustrative and visceral a characterization of the town as any I can think of. Did I mention that this trio of businesses operated one door down from the police department, which surely must have kept a skeptical eye on its neighbors? No, I don't think I did.

Actually, there's a third reason, too: The day before they welcomed me into their home, Annie had attended her first meeting at the Center for an Agricultural Economy as a board member. In this sense, they had become the first of the "old guard" to cross the line and mingle with the agrepreneurs. "I guess I just got tired of getting mad at them and decided to join from the inside," Annie told me. She offered a soft chuckle, but she wasn't really joking. Inside the co-op, along aisles crowded with organic potato chips and hand-dipped candles, there'd been plenty of talk, most of it not very flattering, about these noisy new champions of local food. Some of this might be chalked up to simple sour grapes: The stories that had appeared in the mainstream media had carried scant mention of the co-op. It was a bitter irony that the very business that had laid the foundation for so much of what had come to pass had itself been passed over in the rush to quote the ever-quotable Tom Stearns. The co-op didn't have a Tom Stearns; it had never attempted to market itself in any sort of premeditated way. It was simply there, offering its services to the people of the region. It did not imagine itself as savior or saint; like Ralph and Cindy Persons, or Forrest Foster, or Surfing Veggie Farm, it just did the job it felt most suited to do and took some measure of satisfaction from the knowledge that this job strengthened the community. "Their vision is so much larger than we ever dreamed of," Annie said of the agrepreneurs. Her dark eyes, which can appear sad even as she displays her cheerful disposition, looked thoughtful. "We just wanted to escape society. I think we're all on the same page on how to make this a better planet, but they make it sound like there was nothing here before."

The couple met in 1980, when both worked on a field crew for Hardwick Organic Produce, the first organic vegetable farm in the region. Annie was living in a cabin at the time and often rode her horse to work. Louie, sensing a convenient entry point, cultivated an acute interest in all matters equine. Annie had been raised in Washington, DC, during the height of the antiwar movement and, feeling disillusioned with the city and the people who lived there, fled to attend Sterling College, a small school in Craftsbury that specializes in sustainable agriculture. She was immediately smitten with the region. "I was always really shy as a kid, so coming to a place where someone would smile and beep their horn and wave . . . ," she trailed off. "It just felt like people cared."

Louie's path to Hardwick was more circuitous. Born into a navy family in 1945, he spent his youth in and around New York City as his father followed transfer orders. He was a member of the inaugural class at Southampton College on Long Island; he flunked out, got snagged by the draft, and soon—albeit unwillingly—found himself following in his father's military boot tracks. He became a helicopter pilot and shipped out to Vietnam, an experience that, not surprisingly, shaped his view of the world and how he moves upon it. Mostly, it instilled in him a preference for the slow, thoughtful life. "People sometimes give me a hard time because I sort of plod along," he told me in a quiet voice that indeed seemed a bit plodding. His lean face was framed by a wily hedge of gray hair that matched his beard. "But I have so many friends who were in Nam and relive those experiences every day. I've been so lucky. There are angels flying around me all the time."

Louie put those angels to the test shortly after leaving Vietnam; he took a job with the band Grand Funk Railroad ("We're an American band / We're coming to your town, we'll help you party it down / We're an American band") in a loosely defined role that largely consisted of keeping the train on its wobbly tracks. "I was the mother, girlfriend, sister, brother, and best man at the weddings. It was basically my job to be responsible without getting in the way of the fun." Indeed, Louie did assist with the partying down, though he had the foresight to leave the band's fold when things got serious. "Coke was just starting to blossom, so I figured it was a good time to get out," he says. Off he went to England, to "surf and chill and drink beer" and, occasionally, grab a few days' work on a farm, pitching hay. Eventually, he returned to the States to care for his ailing mother, and after she died in 1978, he packed up his Volvo and headed north, landing a job at a ski resort in central Vermont. During the summers, he worked on a dairy farm to support his developing skiing habit. "This was when the hippie types were just starting to show up and NOFA [the Northeast Organic Farming Association] was starting. One day I was driving the tractor and said, 'That's it: I'll be a vegetable farmer. Then I can take off in the fall and surf and drink beer.'" Arguably, it's been slightly more complicated than that, although it's worth noting that I first met Louie in October when he was standing at the bar in Claire's. He was drinking beer and had recently returned from a day of surfing along the New Hampshire coast.

By the time Louie and Annie met, she'd already been working at the co-op for nearly five years, having been hired only a month after it first opened its doors in 1975. Its approaching 35th anniversary makes the Buffalo Mountain Food Co-op one of the oldest operating food cooperatives in the country. Like most of the co-ops I've visited, it casts a cramped, funky vibe, with well-worn hardwood floors and short, narrow aisles lined with overstacked shelves. Its quarterly member newsletter is called the *Bullsheet*, and it carries articles with titles like "Tails from the Barnyard; or, Manure I Have Known" and "Another Reason for Schools to Ban Genetically Engineered Foods." In the words of the co-op itself, its mission is "to develop within its area of influence a community-owned and -operated, health-oriented, thriving enterprise; to continually educate the community as a whole in regard to food politics, health issues, and our social-cultural activities; to demonstrate alternative approaches to structuring our work environment so that it is more decent and compassionate; to offer healthy, pro-active choices; and to open our doors to, and develop all aspects of our community." The Buffalo Mountain Food Co-op currently has about 1,000 members, each of whom pays annual dues of $12 per adult. For your $12, you're entitled to a 2 percent discount and allowed to vote at the membership meetings, and, technically, you can call yourself part-owner of the co-op. By committing to doing an hour of work per month per household adult, you become a working member and boost your discount to 10 percent. It's actually a pretty damn good deal, particularly if you spend a significant chunk of your food dollars at the co-op and don't mind popping in every so often to pass a hour or two chopping cheese or filling tubs of peanut butter.

The Buffalo Mountain Food Co-op no longer shares a roof with purveyors of firearms and firewater; in the early '90s it moved to its current storefront on Main Street, after the owner of the building and the gun store refused to renew its lease. (Was he concerned about the co-op's influence over his core clientele?) The co-op settled into its new location smoothly and, along with Benny's, two doors up the street, quickly became an anchor for downtown and for local farms like Louie and Annie's own Surfing Veggie and that of Bruce Kaufman and Judy Jarvis over at Riverside, a 30-acre vegetable farm a few miles down the road in East Hardwick. It was a cozy network of producer and purveyor, and no one made much money, which only made it feel cozier and perhaps more just. "Our generation still has that commie, hippie-dippie thing," Annie said.

"Not commie like failed communist," Louie interjected. He'd been sitting quietly, farting intermittently and letting Annie do most of the talking, but now he leaned forward. "More like 'Why do we have to exchange money at all?'"

Still, the years clicked by, and the Buffalo Mountain Food Co-op grew in a slow, steady, and pretty much unintentional way. A few percent more sales each year, a few more members. In the especially good years, when profits ran to $5,000 or $6,000, or even $7,000, the store would run a weeklong supersale for its members. "You can vaporize seven grand pretty quick," Annie said. She chuckled and stated the obvious: "No one in our store knows how to run a business. It just somehow works."

There are probably innumerable reasons why this is true, but I'll start with the most obvious: The Buffalo Mountain Food Co-op is not really about food. I realize that might sound ridiculous; after all, the store now sells $1.5 million worth of the stuff every year; you can hardly turn around in the place without bumping into a stack of organic, free-range, whole-grain something or other. But the prevailing sense, even as you check the items off your list and make your way to one of the two cash registers at the front of the store, is that this isn't so much a place to do commerce, but a place to gather, to meet around shared ideals of what it means to function as a stable community in a precarious world. It is a third place. Perhaps this shouldn't come as a surprise; after all, the Buffalo Mountain Food Co-op's mission statement lays it out in black and white: "to open our doors to and develop all aspects of our community."

To be sure, there are hundreds of food cooperatives throughout this nation, many of which have probably crafted similarly ambitious all-inclusive mission statements. And maybe all of those co-ops are as vibrant as Buffalo Mountain, providing the sort of educational resources and social refuge that Buffalo Mountain provides. In addition to the *Bullsheet*, the co-op organizes a quarterly "community learning exchange" in which community members lead workshops and informal gatherings devoted to, well, pretty much anything. The fall 2008 learning exchange featured 29 options, ranging from an "earth- and lime-plastering workshop" ("an old European technique that uses natural material—lime, sand, manure, and water—for a finish that lasts ages!"), to "indoor composting with red wigglers" (run by the Whacky Worm Sisters), to "women's wellness through dance" ("learn basics and to move beyond the basics while acknowledging the healing that can happen dancing in a community of women"). Remember, we're talking about a tiny food cooperative in a rural town of 3,200. It's worth noting that the calendar of events for the Hunger Mountain Co-op, which is located in Vermont's capitol city of Montpelier and is at least 10 times the size of Buffalo Mountain, isn't nearly as ambitious. "We're really good networkers," Annie told me. "That's what we do best: make connections."

In 2005, on the day after Thanksgiving, the building south of the co-op suffered an electrical fire. The flames never actually touched the co-op, but the water supplied by the 13 (13!) small-town fire departments that responded to the blaze created a mudslide that cascaded off the hill behind the store, smashed through the back wall, and flooded the space with four inches of silt. Hundreds of co-op members pitched in and within a week, the store reopened in a diminished capacity; in February, operations were temporarily moved to—oh, blessed irony—the same building that had once housed a certain gun shop and liquor store. The co-op's management team had budgeted two days for the move, but so many members showed up that it took only a few hours. Flush with insurance money, the co-op completed an extensive renovation of its Main Street space, ripping up six layers of flooring to repair sagging joists and rebuilding walls that had become so rotten that the plate-glass windows were literally sinking into the wood.

And that's where it sits today, although the business is slowly outgrowing the renovated space. In fact, the co-op just underwent another expansion, building a small storage and meeting space into the same steep hillside that once sent soil and water crashing through the building's rear wall.

In February, I found myself crawling behind the co-op café's dishwasher, putty knife in hand, scraping a years-old accumulation of leaked dish soap off the floor. I'd arrived at eight o'clock on a snowy morning to report for two hours of working-member duty. Rachel, the blonde, fast-talking café manager, had forgotten that I was scheduled to work, which wasn't too surprising, because scheduling my hours hadn't necessitated my talking to anyone: I'd simply penned my name onto a sheet of paper posted near the cash register.

"What should I do?" I asked, and Rachel, looking slightly flummoxed, asked if I knew how to make miso soup. I did not; I had not, in fact, ever made a pot of miso soup over the nearly four decades that have comprised my life, but that was nothing I was going to admit to my new boss. "Sure," I said, and it must have sounded like I meant it, because Rachel handed me a pot and a knife, directed my attention to the small bins of prechopped vegetables (onions and carrots seemed like they belonged; I wasn't so sure about the mushrooms and cabbage, but I threw them in anyway), and left to procure a slab of tofu (apparently a key ingredient) from the walk-in cooler. And I started making my first batch of miso soup.

I understood the appeal of being a working member immediately, and it had nothing to do with the 10 percent discount I was earning on my future food purchases. Because frankly, it was fun. How many restaurants could I walk into and immediately be handed the reins to a soup of my own devising, which in a few hours would go on sale to the general public as "Ben's Miso Soup"? (That was Rachel's title; I would never have put my name on the stuff, and if you happened upon a bowl of it, my sincere apologies.) For a couple of hours, I got to play chef and then, just as that started to feel something like work, I got to crawl under the dishwasher, which was actually kind of okay in the way that unpleasant tasks can be fun if you're doing them for someone else and know that you can get up and walk away at any point. Not that you would, but still, it helps. I got free coffee, too, and I got to stand around a bunch chatting with Rachel and Deb, another of the café's regular employees, and I got to listen to the banter as folks came and went, grabbing a drink or one of the chocolate chip scones Deb had just pulled from the oven. I learned that Rachel and her husband, Patrick, were moving onto Louie and Annie's land to farm an acre of mixed vegetables and perhaps erect a yurt. I learned that there were three cats living inside one of the walls of the new addition, and that it was proving exceedingly difficult to extract them. I learned that the café does $200 to $300 worth of business on a good day, and I tried briefly to do the math on that, but it didn't seem very promising, so I stopped.

But mostly, I confirmed what I already knew: that being a member, or even a regular patron, of the Buffalo Mountain Food Co-op isn't merely about the discount and the food you buy with that discount. These are just excuses—worthy excuses, but excuses nonetheless—to come together with like-minded folk in a scruffy little town and celebrate your community in the best way possible: by participating in it. In this sense, the co-op is really just a microcosm of the larger Hardwick ag movement, or at least what the larger Hardwick ag movement might look like eventually; it is rooted in food and provides an outlet for communal engagement and citizen democracy (all co-op members have input and voting rights). It invites and encourages anyone in the community to participate, although it's worth noting that, like most food cooperatives, its member base isn't exactly a reflection of the community as a whole. You can't buy cigarettes at the co-op, or Cheez Whiz or Miracle Whip. There are no Pringles, no Corn Pops, no Little Debbie Snack Cakes. You can't get ground chuck on sale for $.99 a pound or chicken parts for $1.19. In other words, the co-op simply doesn't sell the sort of food that 90 percent of Hardwick eats on a regular basis.

This is not to suggest it should, of course. Its mission isn't to develop all aspects of our community *at the expense of its physical health*. Which means that the co-op's popularity will likely be forever constrained by the dietary habits of the greater Hardwick community in the same way that the region's larger food movement will be, at least until circumstances force the wider population to reconsider the sources of its nourishment. Still, I think it's remarkable just how successful the co-op has become. Think about it: It serves a town of 3,200 and a broader community of perhaps 8,000. And it boasts 1,000 members. That's a phenomenal rate of membership in a region that's not exactly lousy with the sort of overeducated, upper-middle-class, latte-sipping consumers that typically frequent health food stores.

I finished scraping underneath the dishwasher just as the clock struck 10:00, signaling the end of my work commitment for the day. I put away the scraper, mopped up the caked, gloppy mess, and pushed the dishwasher back into place. As I turned to grab a sweater I'd taken off in the heat of my task, I noticed a small, laminated placard lying on the counter. It was, I kid you not, a recipe for miso soup. Miso, water, ginger, garlic, onions, carrots, mushrooms, tofu, seaweed, love. I'd come close, I really had, and this made me feel inordinately happy. But I wasn't finished: I walked over to my pot of soup and held my open hand over it, palm down. Was this how one added love to soup? I wasn't sure, but I figured it couldn't hurt to try.

CHAPTER FIFTEEN

A few days after my adventure with miso, I met Tom Stearns at Claire's for a late-afternoon beer. When I'd called him to arrange the meeting, he had been in a state of high agitation, even when measured against the exuberance to which I'd become accustomed. He'd been invited to speak at a conference of organic farmers in Toronto, he told me, and the trip, which was to commence the next day, was starting to look like a humdinger. "Those damn Canadians are so damn crazy," he said. "I'm getting invites to an insane number of parties. I hope I can hold it together." He let loose a braying laugh.

That wasn't all. An abandoned inn in Greensboro, a majestic place atop a hill, that recently had gone into foreclosure had just been sold at auction to a woman who wanted to operate it in a fashion that might advance the local food movement by offering a curriculum of workshops and tours, all designed around the study of decentralized food production and systems. There was also the possibility of utilizing the space to host visiting troupes of local food advocates from distant communities. There was more, too: Two of Hardwick's most prominent abandoned buildings, vacant for years, had just been purchased. And a distillery was opening in town; it would produce mead and medicinal tinctures from Vermont honey. Things were picking up steam. "My god," shrieked Tom. "This is so fucking amazing. This is one of those things that could just transform the area." I'd heard this line perhaps a dozen times, always in relation to one ag-based development or another, so I didn't pay much attention. But he wasn't finished. "We're gonna look back on this time and say, 'Those were the years this shit went viral.'"

On this account, I was certain he was right, because I could feel it, too. It wasn't just Hardwick; it was everywhere. For a time, I'd worried that the financial crisis, its toll on the economy, and the subsequent drop in energy prices would relieve some of the pressure on food prices and issues of security. Instead, even as the prices of oil and corn disappeared from the headlines, it seemed to trigger a deeper shift, a desire to turn inward and immerse oneself in the fundamentals of life. The particulars of the "nonnegotiable" American way of life suddenly felt wide open to discussion; an entire culture was adrift, cut loose from the tethers of easy credit and, in far too many cases, the employment that had allowed that credit to be serviced. So much of what we'd built our lives on—the sprawling houses, the SUVs, the entertainment systems, the iPhones—had come to feel illusory and misbegotten, and it had happened in only a few short months. There was a sense that the world was shifting on its axis in ways that begged introspection and the humbling acknowledgment that things often unfold in uncomfortable and unpredictable ways. In a way, this shift wasn't so different from the back-to-the-land movement that had brought Annie Galliard and Louie Pulver to the Hardwick area and begat the Buffalo Mountain Food Co-op.

The desire to connect with something real and lasting was showing up everywhere. A few days before Tom and I met at Claire's, Ross Connelly, the publisher of the *Hardwick Gazette*, had written an articulate and thoughtful editorial decrying the lack of democratic participation in Hardwick and drawing parallels between the need for sustainable food systems and our ability to sustain our democracy. "The focus of the agricultural efforts has a decidedly economic bent, which is needed and understandable, and the sense of community inherent in the movement is welcome," Connelly wrote. "The energy and effort directed toward the above endeavors, however, does not appear to include a drive to get involved—to become engaged—in governance." I understood what Connelly was saying, and not for the first time, I imagined how smoothly someone like Tom Stearns or Andrew Meyer might slip into an official governing role. I wondered how that might play out.

Indeed, as time had passed, I'd begun to think more about how things might unfold from here, even as I struggled to answer questions that seemed not to have any answers. Affordability, scale, accessibility, inclusiveness: Whatever expectations I'd had of reaching infallible conclusions to these issues had pretty much evaporated. Still, there was a side benefit to this quandary. Over the months of my reporting, I'd cultivated empathy for everyone involved. Andrew Meyer was trying to get it right, just as Steve Gorelick and Suzanna Jones were trying to get it right, just as the Toms were trying to get it right. However these visions varied, however the focus might be adjusted to fit individual notions of how a community and the food system within that community should function, there were commonalities to them that were stronger than any of them probably realized: the desire to move away from something that has no future and the foresight to understand just how essential this work is.

Too, I was encouraged by some of the talk coming out of the Center for an Agricultural Economy (CAE). Exactly what role this organization—which Andrew Meyer had founded in 2004 as the Center for a Bio-Based Economy—might play had been largely unclear to me, perhaps because it wasn't exactly clear to the people involved in it. I'd heard words like "facilitate" and "convene," and I'd heard the spots the CAE had purchased on the local public radio station that talked about "reinventing a local food economy" or something like that, which sounded nice enough, if a bit presumptive at this early date. Nonetheless, I couldn't quite figure out how the CAE fit into Hardwick's emerging food system.

But in August 2008, the CAE did something that was eminently tangible: It purchased a 15-acre chunk of prime agricultural land only a few blocks from downtown Hardwick. A hundred years ago, the property, known as Atkins Field, had been at the nexus of the town's granite industry; now, only a trio of listing sheds and innumerable chunks of discarded granite remained as evidence of the era. Two of the sheds contained the rusting relics of processing equipment. The other had served as a loading shed; train tracks ran through its center for the entirety of its 400-foot length, and the weathered boards that formed the underside of the roof were blackened by the smoke that had belched from the huge steam locomotives. I know this because Tom Stearns led me there, squeezing through the gap between the large, locked doors at the shed's southern end. "Look at this place," he said after we'd pushed through the opening. "Isn't this place just unbelievable?" He held up his arms, as if the cavernous space were a prize on a TV game show. It *was* unbelievable, and it was impossible for me not to imagine the activity that had once occurred in the shed, the hundreds of workers who had spent months and years of their lives under its rafters, hoisting and prodding and winching stone onto the train cars.

The center's plans for Atkins Field include creating an "eco-industrial park," the exact components of which are evolving. Not surprisingly, Tom Stearns has plenty of ideas, which include, but are by no means limited to, offices for the CAE, meeting rooms for educational and community facilitation purposes, an indoor farmers' market and multifarm CSA distribution center, space for agricultural demonstrations and workshops for both home gardeners and producers, a communal composting facility, a pick-your-own blueberry patch, and rental plots on which budding agrepreneurs could launch food-based businesses. To Stearns's way of thinking, almost anything rooted in small-scale, decentralized ag is fair game, as long as a certain degree of fiscal forward-thinking is applied. "I can tell you what it's not going to be: It's not going to be someone saying, 'Can I grow and cut a half-acre of hay with a scythe so I can go out and not make any money?'" I was a bit taken aback: I'd never heard Stearns use so many "nots" in one sentence.

But despite Tom Stearns's ambition for the space, there'd been a lot of talk about how the Atkins Field project might provide an opportunity to engage the broader Hardwick community in a way that had thus far been lacking, and I found this heartening. The sense that the town's agrepreneurial movement was being driven by a few was palpable, and I'd heard it posited that if the CAE were going to facilitate anything, that thing should be an open community forum. The incredible flurry of media coverage had delivered a powerful boost to the recent efforts of some businesses, but it had also undermined the movement among the local skeptics. Even to me, and I live beyond Hardwick's town line by a good half-dozen miles, it seemed as if the town's future was being mapped out by a few, and that the map was being broadcast to the world before it had been shared—or even discussed—with the other locals.

So it was probably a good thing that the media rush on Hardwick had quieted a bit. The town and its people weren't accustomed to living in the spotlight, and although the coverage was an essential part of getting the story out, of beginning to deliver on the promises of inspiration and process, it seemed to me that a period of retrenchment was in order. Even Stearns, with his mastery of the pitch and his status as resident media whore, acknowledged as much in a quiet moment: "I think what we need is a focused project that meets our mission and also executes really well." Of course, this was merely one way to say that, despite the reams of press, the photographers, and the nominations, there still *hadn't* been a focused project that had met the mission and also executed really well.

Actually, there was plenty going on: A partnership between the CAE and the University of Vermont (UVM) was gaining steam, providing access to just the sorts of resources it would take to develop the types of focused projects Stearns was mulling over. Over the holidays, Stearns and the CAE had presided over an effort called Pies for the People, for which UVM students had gathered to glean squash from High Mowing's fields, processed it in Pete Johnson's big-ass kettle, and baked it into 60 pies—utilizing local maple syrup and eggs, natch—in the kitchen at Sterling College. The pies were distributed to needy families in the region. In December, the CAE had received a $3,500 donation expressly for the purpose of purchasing locally produced food to be distributed by the Hardwick Area Food Pantry, which, like food pantries throughout the state, was dealing with the double whammy dealt by a bereft economy: declining donations and increasing need. The Highfields Center for Composting continued to foster connections with local businesses; in early 2009, the Grand Union supermarket began shipping its food scraps to the composting site, each week diverting as much as a ton of compostable material from the waste stream and saving the market thousands of dollars in annual garbage collection fees. With the savings, the store was considering adding an employee. The local schools were in on the game, too; food-scrap bins had been installed in the cafeterias and students were being taught the art and science of composting. Maybe Tom Gilbert was right; maybe compost was the biggest stick with the most leverage after all.

These were all substantive, successful steps forward, and it occurred to me that any single one of them might have fallen under the headings of focused, true to mission, and well executed if not for one thing: Expectations—those of the community, the media, and even the agrepreneurs themselves—had been elevated to some pretty serious heights.

But even if Tom Stearns fretted over his pint glass that he and the agrepreneurs had failed to meet the inflated expectations they'd helped foster, they were clearly riding a wave during a period when most US industry was smashing into the shore. Part of this was surely due to simple momentum; many of the businesses that comprised the region's agrepreneurial movement were fledging enterprises that were still riding the euphoric wave produced by start-up cash, media attention, and high emotion. To put it bluntly, they had not yet had time to fail.

More charitably, it could be said (*has* been said, in the pages of this very book, in fact) that these ag-based operations enjoy, by the very nature of their commerce, a degree of resilience that the region's car dealers, building-supply centers, and real estate brokers simply can't lay claim to. Economic vibrancy and stability have always been two of the purported hallmarks of local food systems; now, it seems, the folks steering Hardwick's agricultural renaissance find themselves presented with a golden opportunity to prove it's so. The fact that they have, in conjunction with the media, set expectations so high probably won't make this task any easier, because anything less than what's been promised (which, with only modest exaggeration, seems to be nothing less than total agricultural sovereignty, economic vitality, communal pride and stewardship, and perfect health), could be mistaken for failure.

Given the headlines of late 2008 and early 2009, it's no surprise that the economic-vitality portion of that promise was on everyone's mind. That's why I'd coerced Stearns to the bar at Claire's in the first place: I wanted to press him on the specifics of how the agricultural movement he was championing would benefit the region's economy, and how the Atkins Field project might lend the movement a greater sense of inclusiveness. He'd just returned from the gathering of organic growers in Ontario; as expected, it had been a rather boisterous three days and nights. ("Those Canadians are freakin' crazy," he told me. I could only imagine what they were saying about him.) He was feeling a little under the weather, although not enough, apparently, to stop him from draining two pints in rapid succession as he worked through the talking points of what he termed his "resiliency riff."

According to Stearns, there are four legs to the economic-stability table. "Part one is the potential for these businesses to become the Google of Hardwick," Stearns told me. He calls this the "outside-angel-fixes-the-community model," by which the region's ag-based enterprises become so profitable that they are essentially able to shower the town with philanthropy. Or, as Stearns puts it: "This is where me and Pete and Andrew and Mateo get so fucking rich that we can pay for anything the town needs."

I was somewhat alarmed by this particular vision, which I didn't view as a very healthy example of how a decentralized food system might benefit its region, so I was relieved when Stearns continued, "I don't see this as a very good model. It's disempowering. It's like driving to the top of a mountain in Honduras and dropping off 50 typewriters and calling home to brag about how you're teaching literacy." This is not to say that it should be abandoned altogether: Whether it's donating to the food bank or sponsoring events, there is room for philanthropy in Hardwick or any community, as long as it doesn't happen in a vacuum or at the expense of others.

Part two of Stearns's local-ag-as-economic-driver model charges these businesses with the responsibility for educating employees on the critical importance of keeping their paychecks in the community. "I'm putting $25,000 to $30,000 into people's pockets every two weeks," he said. He was talking about the payroll at High Mowing Organic Seeds. "If we're doing things right as a business, they are making choices to eat at Claire's, shop at the co-op, and buy gas at the local station. If you can show people that spending money locally has a positive effect, it has much greater impact than telling them that shopping at Wal-Mart is bad. Maybe it's sexier to fight against things, but in the long term, it doesn't work as well."

Too, Stearns believes that as Hardwick's business district is propelled into permanent orbit around agriculture, the mission and mores of the individual enterprises will infect the region with the "buy local" message. "If you work at a dollar store selling crap from China, is supporting your local economy going to be drilled into your head? Probably not. But if you work at High Mowing Organic Seeds or Vermont Soy or Pete's Greens, you can be damn sure it is."

The third of Tom Stearns's agriculture business edicts is to develop key metrics by which to measure and grade success (or the lack thereof). The specific components of these metrics have yet to be determined—and even debated in great detail—but they might include:

- The percentage of total jobs in the region that are ag-based
- The average wage of these jobs
- The percentage of locally produced products that stay in the region
- The percentage of wages paid by these ag-based employers that remain in the region
- The amount of waste Hardwick's ag system generates and what percentage of that waste is reclaimed
- The percentage of local land that's available for agricultural purposes and how that relates to local needs in regard to food production and consumption
- The availability of loans and other forms of capital for ag-related endeavors
- The level of social awareness, such as how many people in the region believe that implementing and supporting a local food system is a worthy endeavor

"I want to own the back page of the *Hardwick Gazette* and have it be an ongoing forum for educating the community about local food systems," Stearns said. "How much could the back page cost—$250? My god, think of all the good stuff we could do for $250 a week."

Part four concerns strategic products. "There are certain ag-based products that, if you run through all the scenarios—$50 per barrel oil, $200 per barrel oil, a crashing economy, a booming economy—will always make sense," explained Stearns. "One key metric is the shipping cost relative to the value; that number has to—*has to*—be under 10 percent." In other words, according to Tom Stearns, if it costs $10 to ship $80 worth of product, you've got problems.

Stearns continued, perhaps a bit smugly: "Seeds win on all accounts. When people feel rich, they garden for leisure. When they feel poor, they garden for economy. My shipping-cost-to-value ratio is about 4 percent, which means I've got a lot of wiggle room to absorb rising shipping costs. And damn it, I just feel good about selling them!" He took a long pull from his pint; a few bubbles of beer foam stuck to his beard.

Stearns will be the first to admit that he didn't do much strategizing when he launched High Mowing Organic Seeds; the business simply grew out of his love for seeds and his fervent entrepreneurial spirit, and it might well be considered dumb luck that his passions fit within the parameters of his resiliency riff. But in the face of economic rules that are being rewritten at an unparalleled pace, newer ag-based businesses (or any business, for that matter) may not have the luxury of dumb luck. Even among Hardwick's ag sector, it's not difficult to identify businesses that might suffer in a downturn. Consider soy milk: It's heavy, which damages its shipping-cost-to-value ratio. Compared with its thirst-quenching alternatives (water, cow's milk, and Bud Light, the last of which is admittedly disadvantaged as a companion to break-fast cereal), it's expensive, which hurts its chances in a depressed economy, and the infrastructure to produce it requires significant up-front investment. Much the same could be said of artisanal cheese, although the high price of the cheddars and blues emerging from Jasper Hill's cellar helps tilt the shipping-cost-to-value ratio in its favor; currently, Jasper Hill pays an average of 26 cents to ship a pound of cheese that wholesales for about $10, giving them an enviable 2.6 percent shipping-cost-to-value ratio. But can the consumer's appetite for $20-per-pound blue cheese hold up in a recession? Or even a depression? Can the Kehlers keep up with their debt obligations if sales stall? Even High Mowing Organic Seeds, an established, decade-old business that's in the midst of 60 percent year-over-year growth, isn't pulling down a profit.

It should be noted that neither Stearns nor I is making specific predictions regarding any of Hardwick's agrepreneurial businesses. I am not an economist, and I don't place much faith in the so-called dismal science to begin with (remember when most economists were confidently proclaiming the subprime mortgage crisis was "contained"?). All the same, it's quite possible that not all of the region's ag-based businesses will emerge from the economic tumult unscathed. The notion that local food systems are more resilient to economic hardship is compelling, but still largely untested. "I certainly would like it to be the case," said Shermain Hardesty, the cooperative extension specialist in the department of agricultural and resource economics at the University of California at Davis. "But I can't unequivocally say it's true." Hardesty is currently conducting two studies that should help define the economic resilience of local food systems, but she says it's simply too early to draw any definitive conclusions. The verdict will be rendered by consumers voting with their dollars: "The externalities of the industrial food system are just starting to become acknowledged by more people. Once we start to quantify the costs, we start to realize that industrial food isn't really that cheap."

In other words, here we are back at the cost issue again, with your so-called average American food consumers trying to figure out how to keep the kiddies fed in an era of declining wages. Are they willing to consider the externalities Hardesty speaks of? Do they even know such externalities exist? Or are they simply going to fill their shopping carts based on the same set of priorities that's always dictated their food shopping: price, convenience, and taste buds that have been bludgeoned by additives with such frequency that unadulterated foods have been rendered nearly tasteless. In other words, perhaps it's not merely that many Americans think they can't afford local foods or find them inconvenient. It's that they don't *like* them.

For his part, Stearns isn't overly concerned that he doesn't have specific answers to these questions. His faith in the willingness and ability of Hardwick to embrace the local food economy he's working so hard to foster is predicated on an even deeper faith: that the forces converging on us will have a deep and abiding impact, rendering the positive aspects of the food renaissance he is steering self-evident. "The universe, or whatever metaphysical thing you want to call it, is inviting me into something," he told me that night at Claire's. I was a bit taken aback by his language; I'd never heard him speak in anything but the pragmatic vernacular of agriculture and economy. "I don't mean to be new age-y about it, but the way multiple things are aligning . . . " For a moment, he struggled to explain himself. A long pull from his pint seemed to focus his thoughts. "There are big, big factors in the world converging right now that are pushing all this stuff to the top. I'm just glad to be part of it."

But what, exactly, is he a part of? Is the Hardwick agrepreneurial revolution truly a leading indicator for the way things will soon be for everyone, everywhere? Will it thrive in Hardwick (and will Hardwick thrive in its presence), but remain an anomaly to the entrenched industrial food system, with its enormous economy of scale, political might, and fantastically deep marketing pockets? Or might it die on the vine before it has a chance to prove itself?

At times, in the midst of all the excitement or in the presence of Tom Stearns's irrepressible optimism, it is hard to remember that what's happening in Hardwick is still largely untested. Stearns knows it feels right, and he is prepared to make arguments based on these emotions. And maybe that's enough; maybe it's perfectly reasonable to align ourselves with whatever metaphysical thing is compelling Stearns to commit every fiber of his being to Hardwick's ag revolution. Could it be that the emotions and instinct that are telling us to believe in decentralized agriculture are stronger, healthier indicators than any numeric formula we can devise? We've gotten to this crossroads by believing only in numbers, and those numbers have told us that growing more food for less money on less land is a worthy pursuit. If our faith in the simple economics of food can lead us so far astray, should we really be judging the viability of our food systems by percentages of this, that, and the other?

Ultimately, we probably *do* need these numbers; we live in a culture that believes, deeply, in the language of facts and figures. If we are to convince the bankers to loan us money and the politicians to support this cause, we're going to need to speak their languages. This is not to say that we cannot introduce new terminology to the conversation. Imagine a world in which lenders base their decisions on factors such as soil health, water quality, and percentage of waste that's composted. Imagine legislation that creates tax incentives for farmers to sell directly to consumers or, vice versa, compels consumers to keep their food dollars in their communities. Are these things really so far-fetched?

Tom Stearns doesn't think so. I don't think so. Still, there is a real risk in creating the metrics Stearns talks about. What if, according to these specific definitions of success, Hardwick's agrepreneurs fail? What if the metaphysical thing Stearns speaks of doesn't really translate? Tom Stearns and anyone who believes in the power of decentralized food systems would do well to prepare themselves for these possibilities.

By dint of its location near the center of town, by dint of its size (15 acres in a town of 3,200 is a significant piece of property), and by dint of the lack of a profit motive, Atkins Field could prove to be the ideal vector for delivering Hardwick's agricultural economy to the general populace and seeding the new terminology of success. The only problem: How to go about it? The CAE could convene and facilitate to its heart's content, but it isn't hard to imagine such efforts devolving into a metaphoric food fight over the specifics of the Atkins Field vision. "This is a great opportunity to engage the public," Tom Gilbert told me when I asked him about it. Gilbert is a director of the CAE and, of all the protagonists of Hardwick's ag revolution, the most articulate about matters of community building. "I want to see that project designed as much as possible by the community, but to do that we're going to have to have a very organized, facilitated process or it will just be a mess." We were talking in the Highfields office on a frigid January day; he wore a T-shirt bearing an iconic image of Earth taken from space and held his one-year-old daughter, Thea.

All of which suggested to me that the stakes for the Atkins Field project are very high. In the absence of any real dialogue with the citizenry of Hardwick, Atkins Field provides an ideal entry point. And let's be honest: If Hardwick's food system is to fulfill the long-heralded promise of local food systems—that they can nourish and sustain communities in ways far broader and deeper than the simple act of forking food into mouths—then the town's citizenry must be engaged. The Center for an Agricultural Economy and all the folks working so hard to breathe life into this new way of imagining how our food is produced and distributed will never fully realize their vision without engaging the populace. Not every single one of Hardwick's 3,200 residents needs to come on board; indeed, it would be naive idealism to believe that even a modest majority of the population will care enough to make their voices heard. But thus far it had almost felt as if there'd been something of an end run around the very people who stood to gain the most from this movement, and I'd begun to believe that the root of many of the criticisms being voiced was embedded in the fertile soil of this fact. "We needed to communicate to our people first," Tom Gilbert said, when I asked what he thought of my theory. "To communicate to the world first is just the wrong order." He was talking about the spate of national media coverage. "It's not going to be that every single person in Hardwick comes to our meetings or even pays attention, but they've gotta feel like they've got a dog in the fight. Transferring information is one of the most important things we need to do." Then, because he couldn't help it, he slipped into the language of nonprofits: "People don't need to be told what to do; they need to be empowered with information. It's about awakening that sense of capacity that's part of everyone. Creating a healthy food system is an ideal way to awaken and leverage that capacity." In other words, this is damn important work, the stakes are very high, and we need to get people off their asses, now. Or something like that.

It is likely to be quite some time before Atkins Field evolves into whatever vision is imagined for it. The so-called eco-industrial park will require significant investments in resources both financial and physical at a time when the former is increasingly difficult to come by. The facilitating and convening processes that will ostensibly predate the groundbreaking have barely begun. If you drove to Hardwick now, turned down Granite Street, and parked next to the old loading shed, you'd probably see pretty much what I saw: a broad stretch of grass dotted with the littered packaging of exactly the sort of food the agrepreneurs hope to vanquish and a trio of tired-looking buildings that clearly were constructed for a purpose that no longer exists and which weren't honored with the necessary upkeep. The land is used for the town's annual Spring Festival gathering, but otherwise, it's little visited by anyone beyond the occasional walker or picnicking family.

There is something appealingly metaphoric in the history of Atkins Field and its potential to forward Hardwick's food system and connect it to the broader community. This is where, over a century ago, the town's granite industry flourished. This is where much of the region's stone exports were processed and loaded for their final destinations, where the community gathered in the shared labor that would provide for their families and, therefore, the town. Could it again serve the same purpose, only this time with food rather than rock? If so, if it is conceived and structured in a way that is truly inclusive and nonexploitative, if it becomes a concept people can rally around and feel they have a stake in, it might be the best example of how a food system can transform a community in a country that desperately needs such examples.

I thought about another passage in Ross Connelly's powerful editorial:

> There is a certain irony that local government, which is most accessible, is often left to those whose interests lie in maintaining the status quo rather than searching for new ideas to address common needs. Governance is difficult, often draining and damning, but turning one's back on government doesn't make it go away. Waiting for government to follow rather than being willing to be a part of it to see that it leads can drain energy. Ignoring government

leaves a vacuum that will be filled by those who choose to pursue its power—often, for their own narrow ends rather than the common good. Progress comes when there are new ideas put on the table by the people elected to sit at it. Setting an agenda provides direction that a petition seldom does. That which we do in common requires hard work. Just as people's energy enables sustainable agriculture, there is a need for citizen involvement if we are to have sustainable democracy, too.

Could Hardwick's developing food system—indeed, a regionalized food system anywhere—really hold the potential to launch a groundswell of democracy? That's not exactly what Connelly was saying, but the connection was obvious. And the answer, I believe, is yes. For too long, I'd thought of food politics as something that happened on a larger stage. The term had always made me think of subsidies and lobbyists and their steely grip on those in the corridors of political power. I thought about the battles over GMOs, recombinant bovine growth hormone, and the National Animal Identification System, a draconian proposal that would require the identification and tracking of every single piece of livestock in the United States, the onus of which would fall to the farmer. The added burden on small, regional producers, many of whom already tread a gossamer line between solvency and bankruptcy, would be disastrous. In short, I thought of the bureaucracy and regulations that had evolved out of the cozy relationship between the food corporations and our political leadership and how the vast majority of those regulations erected roadblocks to the creation of citizen-led, decentralized food systems. It's not just that we've let our food freedom slip away from us, it's that it's been *taken*.

But just as it's possible to localize food production and distribution, isn't it possible to rescale the politics that will always attach themselves to the most critical, life-giving commerce we know? And if these new food systems are structured to be inclusive, empowering, and sustainable, couldn't the new style of politics they foster share the same principles? The participatory nature of local food systems holds tremendous power, not merely to secure and understand the cycle and source of our nourishment, but to reawaken a sense of responsibility for and toward the communities in which we live. To assume accountability for our food is to assume accountability for our lives. Once coaxed back to life, where will that accountability end? It's anyone's guess, but for the record, mine is that it will prove a far more powerful force than we can even imagine.

"Eating is an agricultural act," Wendell Berry famously wrote in his 1989 essay *On the Pleasures of Eating*. And agriculture, in its capacity to either sustain our every action and thought or to strand us on the wrong side of a broken producer-to-consumer link, is everything. Absolutely everything.

CHAPTER SIXTEEN

At the outset of my reporting on Hardwick's food system, I'd assumed that at some point I'd need to make an accounting of it and measure it against my own admittedly naive understanding of what a healthy food system should look like. It had been many months since I'd laid out my four guidelines for localized, sustainable agriculture: It must offer economic viability to small-scale producers, it must be based on sunshine, it must feed the locals, and it must be circular. Even when I wrote them, it felt rather presumptuous, as if I were claiming to have cracked a code that had eluded thousands of others, most of whom are surely better versed in healthy food systems than I. Hell, in the Hardwick area alone there are literally dozens of folks whose understanding of the issues runs to depths I might never plumb. Some of these people are old enough to be my father; they've been thinking about these things since Wendell Berry and Michael Pollan were snot-nosed kids begging their parents for another lollipop.

There's nothing particularly wrong with those guidelines, and maybe we need the direction they can provide. Weaning ourselves off industrial ag might be common sense, but that doesn't mean we're not flying blind. In 1900, there were 76 million Americans and nearly 30 million farms. Today, there are 307 million Americans and 2 million farms. As empowering as it feels to regain control of our food system, let's not pretend the numbers are in our favor. Let's not pretend we know exactly how this is going to work out.

This much I do know: Hardwick is home to an enviable level of small-scale, circular-minded producers, and the town's residents, while certainly not benefiting from across-the-board equality in regard to access to these producers' goods, are more able to sustain themselves on food grown by their neighbors than perhaps any other community in the United States. That's a pretty big and bold claim itself, but I'd seen enough to be convinced that it was true.

So, yeah, there's a lot of damn good food being produced in the Hardwick, Vermont, region. From a strictly nutritive standpoint, as an antidote to our industrialized diet, Hardwick does its job very, very well, delivering a degree of quality and variety in its food umbrella that rivals the most food-abundant towns in North America, and probably quite a few in Europe, too. Chicken, beef, apples, eggs, lettuce, pork, cheese, tofu, milk, berries, tomatoes, sauerkraut, bread, and, if you count the exotics flowering in High Mowing's test garden, hon tsai tai. I mean, hey, what more could you want? Finances notwithstanding, one could eat from within, say, a 20-mile radius of Hardwick for much of the year. With a modicum of food-preservation skills and the time to ply those skills, it's not hard to imagine eating an entirely Hardwickian diet 365 days per year. You'd want for some salt and perhaps a few pounds of coffee, but you *could* do it.

Which is nice and all, but it's still largely predicated on a dangerous assumption: that the center—the industrial food system—holds. Because it is, after all, the center that still feeds the majority of Hardwick's residents, leaving all those tasty, nutrient-dense local morsels for you and me. And because if the center crumbles, the demand for local food will intensify even as the inputs Hardwick's producers rely on become markedly more expensive and, eventually, scarce, making their prices rise.

A surfeit of damn good, locally produced food in Hardwick (or anywhere else, for that matter), satisfying as it may be, does not food sovereignty make. For that, we need an accounting of the resource base, the interconnectedness of the region's producers, and their viability in the face of the rapidly shifting sands of finance, climate change, fossil-fuel availability, food distribution security—the list goes endlessly and unsettlingly on. If the past few years have taught us anything, it is that the next few years will be fraught with uncertainty. Because it's impossible to know exactly how things will unfold, it is equally impossible to define the exact metrics we should use to make determinations regarding the viability and resilience of Hardwick's producers. So the accounting I sought was not merely an accounting of the volume and variety of the food, which were clearly impressive, but also a measure of the process that was creating the system.

I was presented with an opportunity to take this measure on the first Tuesday of February 2009, when the monthly business-owners' meeting convened at the home of Pete Johnson and Meg Gardner. These meetings, which had been orchestrated and launched by Tom Stearns and Pete Johnson in August 2006, were designed to be informal-yet-confidential affairs in which entrepreneurial peers could come together to discuss everything from problem employees, to the emotional aspects of running a business, to financial issues; since its inception, Tom Stearns told me, members of the 25-strong group had loaned each other more than $300,000, with nothing more than handshakes to seal the deals. The group wasn't limited to Hardwick's agreprenuers—there were members from as much as 90 minutes away—but it was certainly dominated by the region's agricultural CEOs. Tom Stearns was there, as were Andrew Meyer, June Van Houten from the Highfields Center for Composting, Linda Ramsdell from Claire's, and John and Rocio Clark from Applecheek Farm. Every month, the group gathers at a different member's place of business, and the host is required to choose a topic of discussion. The subject of this meeting was of particular interest to me: how to increase local food consumption in Vermont.

By the time I arrived at the old colonial Johnson and Gardner share, the informal, premeeting portion of the meeting was in full swing. Johnson was hacking apart a couple of chickens he'd roasted; the birds had been raised, along with 798 others, in a field behind the house. He wore a red T-shirt with a John Deere logo and looked his usual tousled self. A table was buried beneath potluck contributions, wine bottles, and chocolates (one of the members owns a small chocolate outfit in Stowe). A couch-side table held a copy of the bestselling self-help/inspirational lifestyle book *The 4-Hour Workweek: Escape 9-5, Live Anywhere, and Join the New Rich* (Crown, 2007). I thought this might be a joke, but I wasn't sure. A shelf of CDs contained discs by Joni Mitchell and the Beastie Boys. The lights were on, but a pair of candles burned for atmospheric purposes.

Stearns's beard had grown bushier still in the days since I'd seen him; he angled for me with a beer in his hand and a slightly crazed—which is to say normal for him—expression on his face. "Dude!" he squealed. "Things are going nuts. We've got this thing going with Channel 3 called Grow a Row for the Hungry. I'm going to be on TV like craaaazy!" He did a strange sort of whole-body wiggle, as if trying to contain an alien life force that threatened to burst forth through his forehead, before going on to tell me that January 2009 had been High Mowing's biggest month ever, with sales nearly 70 percent higher than the year prior. I asked how this compared to projections.

"We projected 65 percent growth."

I was surprised by the ambition of such a forecast in the face of a collapsing economy and told him so. Stearns nodded: "I'm an eternal optimist, but I've not really been proven wrong." And then: "I hope that as this house of frickin' cards comes crashing down and all these people have lost their shirts investing in distant corporations, they'll realize that investing in their neighbors is the only way we'll survive with any shred of dignity."

On that note, which left me unsure about whether to feel hopeful or despairing, Johnson called the meeting to order. "I think we're in a time and place to really move forward." He was talking about the local food movement and he leaned forward, resting his forearms on his knees. "I'm as guilty as anyone of sort of assuming that things will always carry on the way they are for the indefinite future. But I'm starting to feel like that's a really dangerous assumption."

There were nods all around, and a brief hush as everyone considered the implications of Johnson's words. We'd all thought about this stuff before, but the words carried a weight no one really wanted to bear. The food crisis had, thus far, been largely a crisis of abstraction and externalities. No one in Johnson and Gardner's living room had gone hungry for even a day; the proof of our riches was balanced on our laps. Chicken and chocolate, corn chips and red wine. The melancholy in considering a future of scarcity isn't merely considering what it might feel like to be truly, deeply hungry; after all, most Americans don't even know how to imagine such a thing, having lived only in abundance. Instead, I think it's the fear of being forced to part with the small luxuries in our lives. We can imagine losing chocolate, and therefore, we fear it. We can't imagine starving, and therefore we don't.

As usual, it was Stearns who disrupted the gathering gloom. "I think a lot about what we need to do this." This was perhaps the understatement of the year. A calculator had appeared on his lap, and he was tapping furiously on its keys. "Let's see, Pete, what do you think? Can you feed 25 families per acre?" He was talking about produce only, not meat and dairy and grains. Johnson shrugged and nodded. More tapping, and Tom had the answer. "A hundred and sixty acres. We'll need 160 acres." A quick accounting of the region's vegetable producers ensued: Johnson, with his 30 acres, Bruce Kaufman and Judy Jarvis at Riverside Farm with their 30 or so acres. David Allen at Hazendale Farm was in for 10, and Louie and Annie for another 5. There were a handful of others, most in the one- to three-acre range. The consensus was surprisingly upbeat:

From a strictly vegetable perspective, assuming not a single green pepper, tomato, or lettuce leaf strayed from the region, Hardwick-area producers could supply the region with perhaps half its vegetable needs for perhaps half the year. This seemed like wonderfully good news, so a congratulatory box of chocolates was passed around the room and talk turned to matters of distribution because, as Stearns put it, "It doesn't make sense for us all to be driving around in our Subarus delivering spinach."

The point of all this is not to deliver a blow-by-blow account of this particular meeting, which would go on to include issues of consumer education ("I prefer to 'invite' people to join us, rather than try to 'educate' them," said Stearns, which made good sense to me), an entirely different kind of retail outlet that might combine local foods with typical convenience-store items such as lottery tickets and light beer ("We need to find a formula that will get the other 95 percent of Hardwick into the store, because they're sure as hell not going to the co-op," noted Meyer), the potential pitfalls of local-food success ("If the buzz generates so much attention [that] we start shipping across the country, that would be very bad"—Stearns again), and the potential for a massive influx of cash courtesy of the Obama stimulus plan ("I think everyone should be prepared for the amount of money we're going to get," said Meyer, who'd been in touch with his Capitol Hill buddies and was feeling quite chipper about the prospects for Hardwick).

Rather, the point is to make two points, really. One, that the variety of businesses represented in Pete and Meg's living room was, in and of itself, an indicator of just how far Hardwick has come and of the potential—admittedly not yet fully realized—for substantive collaboration. Represented in this single room, on the top floor of an old farmhouse in rural Vermont, giddy on wine and beer and chocolate, was the beginning of something circular: compost, seed, and farmer. I'd heard from Stearns that for the first time ever, Johnson had committed to buying the bulk of his seed from High Mowing, and that it would likely be the largest single order in the company's history. "About frickin' time," Stearns told me, and he was being his usual good-natured self, but I could tell that he really meant it. And at the Highfields Center for Composting, I'd seen a plan drafted for Johnson that would allow him to make his own potting soil, at least in part from ingredients supplied by Highfields, which had in turn been collected and distilled from the food and animal waste of the region. In the grand scheme of all things agricultural, these were quiet, almost pitifully small deals, at least when measured in dollars and volume. But of course they represented something much larger indeed: They represented the slow, hard bending of the straight-line ends that characterize our linear agriculture system.

The second point is that these conversations are happening. I'm not about to suggest that Hardwick, Vermont, is the only town where people are gathering to consider an agricultural future very much unlike the present, because I know it's not. Still, I am certain that number is fairly low. In 2000, the US Census recorded 25,375 "places," a loose definition of cities, towns, and counties within our nation's borders. Is it even worth guessing how many of these "places" are home to the sort of convening, calculating, and contemplating I witnessed in Johnson's farmhouse? Could it be even 1 percent, a total of 254 communities? Maybe it could. Maybe. Still, it seems equally likely that it's fewer than that.

Of course, conversation—even considered conversation between well-meaning folks lubricated on free-range chicken and local, organic wine—does not a healthy food system make. And even as I watched this hopeful-sounding debate play out, I was struck by the insular nature of the group and could not help but wonder if a dozen people, no matter how ambitious and forward-thinking, could really exert the sort of transformative change that is so sorely needed. Of course, the answer is no, they can't, but then, no movement starts with the full consensus of the citizenry; it almost always begins with one or two people possessing the necessary degree of insanity to fuel an unrelenting passion that can inspire and pull others into the groundswell of the movement.

What I observed on that cold night in Craftsbury in an old farmhouse owned by a young couple who might well represent the new face of farming in this country was an evolution of the process necessary to take this little, germinating seed of an idea and nurture it into something bigger and more fully realized (yes, I know I'm getting a little carried away with the metaphor, but what the hell). And to my thinking, it is the process as much as—if not more so than—the actual food that will either propel this movement into the mainstream or see it die on the vine (there I go again). Hardwick is Hardwick, unique in its particular resources and individuals. How many of America's 25,375 places are home to a seed producer, a composting operation, and a vegetable grower, all close enough together that they could exchange their goods on horseback? This number, I'm willing to bet, is somewhere in the range of one. And that one is Hardwick.

There are two things that Hardwick can export, two lessons it can teach the 25,374 other places in the United States. The first is exactly the thing I'd dismissed as being too vague at the outset of this book: inspiration. The second is the concrete specifics of the process on which the Hardwick food system is being built, because it is the process that can be ubiquitously applied to the particular resources of a given region. The measure of Hardwick's food system success or failure must, at some point, come to include metrics that can define its impact on the land and community. But it must also be held up against the ability of all its people—not merely those gathered on a certain Tuesday night in a certain farmhouse in February 2009, but its full citizenry—to imagine, implement, and participate in a process that allows the system to flourish in full equality and in the face of converging forces.

I glanced over at Tom Stearns, who was again hammering away at his poor calculator. I must have missed something, because now he looked up and launched into another monologue. "Ninety-five percent of the people around here may not be ready to change completely, but they might be ready to change a little bit. And they get sucked in and we bombard them with local food gospel." He was grinning hugely, clearly relishing the opportunity to meta- phorically bludgeon the masses with heads of organic lettuce and the carcasses of pasture-raised fowl. "It's going to take money; it's going to take lots of money. Millions. But we'll have it. I know we'll have it."

Even in the midst of the deepest economic downturn since the Great Depression, I didn't doubt him for a second.

CHAPTER SEVENTEEN

Spring came near, and the people of Hardwick were ready. It had been a hard winter, marked by the sort of relentless cold that freezes water lines and provokes desperate late-March scrambles for dry firewood. Up on Bridgman Hill, in the fields surrounding the Meyer, Trudeau, and Foster and Shaw farms, the snow seemed unwilling to relinquish its grip on the bare earth, and the thermometer, even in early March, fell below zero. Down at Pete's Greens the greenhouses were warm and lush with new growth, each one a little oasis of summer. At the High Mowing warehouse, seed packets were flying out the door at a frenetic pace and Tom Stearns paced the building, cell phone pressed to his ear, explaining to a reporter in Seattle how Hardwick—gritty, blue-collar, maligned Hardwick—had become a beacon of hope in a world of despair.

In the kitchen at Claire's, Steven Obranovich was trying to use up the last of his canned tomatoes and frozen spinach, eager for the return of both fresh produce and the hordes of diners that summer would bring. Next door at the Center for an Agricultural Economy, director Monty Fischer was fielding phone calls and e-mails from hundreds of people from hundreds of communities who wanted to know exactly what was up with this little town in northern Vermont. One door down from that, in the Buffalo Mountain Food Co-op, the aisles were as crowded as ever and the smell of fresh bread (Charlie Emers, the fast-talking fireplug of a man who owns Patchwork Bakery, had just delivered a still-warm batch) hung in the air like a promise. Across the street, above the Galaxy Bookshop, Tom Gilbert of the Highfields Center for Composting was on the phone, explaining the finer points of on-site composting to a farmer in Lyndonville.

Eight miles to the north, in Walden, Louie Pulver was sorting through his garden tools and plotting the season's first surf session and, more specifically, that weightless moment when his board catches the wave's cresting momentum and delivers him to someplace that is neither here nor there and is, therefore, exactly where he needs to be. Just a bit to the east, down a maple-lined dirt road, Steve Gorelick knelt beside a goat, milking into a small metal bucket and hoping for some sun to charge the batteries that power his family's home.

Over at Vermont Soy, Andrew Meyer was punching numbers, trying to determine how best to maneuver his fledgling business through the worst economic meltdown since the Great Depression.

On the far side of the Lamoille River, across the street from Atkins Field, the community gardens lay fallow, the remnants of last season's crops folded and wilted under the remaining snow. Soon, the dozen or so families who tend the small, riverside plots would be able to turn over the soil, sow a few packets of seed, then wait and hope for the growth that somehow, no matter how many times one sees it happen, always feels like a surprise.

Yes, on so many fronts, it had been a hard winter. For a time, it had seemed as if Vermont might be insulated from the nation's deteriorating economy and then, when it became clear this would not be so, it had seemed as if the state might at least be spared the worst. Then at some point even that notion was exposed as the wishful thinking it was. The governor talked of laying off more than 600 state workers; IBM, Vermont's largest private employer, shed nearly 500. By the end of March, the state's unemployment rate spiked to 7.9 percent, nearly double what it had been when I started writing this book in the fall of 2008.

Predictably, Tom Stearns remained effusively optimistic in the face of bad news. It didn't hurt that his personal star had continued to rise; in early February, he'd been nominated for the Natural Resources Defense Council's Growing Green Award (or, as he so succinctly put it to me in an e-mail, "The Natural Resources Defense Council Greenest Motherfucker Award"), and it seemed as if every other week he was jetting off to deliver the keynote address at one conference or another. He talked about detaching further from High Mowing so he could more fully apply himself to the business of food systems. He talked about the tremendous resilience built into Hardwick's food system, and how that resilience would allow the town to better weather the economic storm. He talked about his efforts to convince Andrew Meyer to sell him an acre of land so that he might become a Hardwick resident and therefore become eligible to run for town office. "I have those aspir . . . interests," he told me. I understood why he'd corrected himself midword. He was beginning to learn where and when to apply the soaring language of ambition and that Hardwick was the sort of town where his "interests" would be better received than his "aspirations." I found this heartening.

On one particularly chilly evening, in the waning light of one of the final, cruel days of this winter that seemed to never want to end, I pushed open the door to Claire's. It had snowed lightly that morning, then warmed to just above freezing, and now the streets of Hardwick carried a wet, drab look that made everything feel disheveled and impoverished. Or perhaps it was just the endless flow of bad news that poured forth from every sector of the economy and every corner of the globe. Whatever was going on out there was gathering a serious head of steam, and people were uneasy. I was uneasy.

It was Kristina's last night as general manager of Claire's. I wasn't privy to the details, and I lacked the courage to press for specifics, but it was clear that it hadn't been an entirely amicable parting. This didn't really surprise me: Launching a restaurant is hard enough without creating an entirely new business model and implementing that model under a five-owner democracy. But it still felt a little sad and, in a small way, like a refutation of everything the Hardwick food model stood for. That's totally irrational and entirely unfair, I realize: Of course there will be tensions. Of course people will move on.

I took the last empty seat at the bar and ordered a pint. Kristina came over; she was in high spirits. At 9:00 p.m., in a little less than two hours, her tenure at Claire's would officially end, and within a week, she told me, she'd be lying on a beach on the Outer Banks of North Carolina. "It's time to get away," she said. "It's *really* time to get away."

The restaurant began to fill up. Andrew Meyer came in, followed in short order by his wife, parents, and brothers. Deb from the co-op café was waiting tables; Rachel from the co-op café was drinking margaritas. Barry from the co-op came in and sat down next to Rachel. Louie Pulver slipped through the door and strolled across the room in his laconic way. Jessie, an occasional waitress at Claire's, was there, sitting at the bar next to Lindsey, another occasional waitress and employee at High Mowing Organic Seeds. Sophia, who does marketing and sales at Vermont Soy, came in. Bill Half, a vegetable grower in Walden, began chatting with Louie and drinking beer. John Clark from Applecheek Farm showed up. He'd just drilled 300 taps into the maple trees on his farm and was hoping for an early sap run. He began talking to Todd Parlo, the proprietor of Walden Heights Nursery. Earlier, Todd had told me that he'd planted upwards of 400 apple trees on his 10 acres. I got into a pig conversation with a fellow named Michael who keeps rare-breed hogs up the road in Greensboro Bend. I thought I might buy one. I ordered another beer from Don, the barkeep. Steven emerged from the kitchen to deliver a plate to someone at the bar. Outside, it had gone completely dark, masking the drabness of the day and, better yet, everything associated with it.

I looked around the room and I realized, not for the first time, but for the first time with such absolute, startling clarity, the incredible, indelible strength of this community and how much of that strength had been forged by food. And also how that strength could connect the disparate forces behind Hardwick's evolving food economy. Wealthy and poor; beef and tofu; Whole Foods in Boston and the Buffalo Mountain Food Co-op two doors down the street; young and old; land barons and tenants; currency of money and currency of community. To suggest that these things will always exist in perfect harmony would be both naive and dishonest. But it is no less naive and dishonest to insist that they must be mutually exclusive, that the ideal is one and not the other.

Sometimes it seems as if I look at Hardwick and think only of how far it has to go. On this night, I looked at Hardwick and thought only about how far it has come. And I realized that for all my struggling to grapple with the particulars of the town's emerging food system, everything that's happened makes perfect sense. It is only the irrationality and incomprehensible complexity of the arrangement we've created that makes it seem as if what is transpiring in Hardwick is something mysterious and maybe even unnatural. To understand that it is not, and that it is, in fact, the only sane response to the fractured vulnerability of our national food culture is this little town's greatest gift to the rest of the world.

It may not be an easy gift to give. I came to this story with the preconceived understanding that Hardwick's agrepreneurial revolution is unambiguously, inarguably beneficial to the community and its people, that decentralized food production and distribution are simple and obvious answers to a complex problem, that the power and potential in food are there for us all, just waiting to be tapped. I still believe these things, but I know now that there's nothing simple about it, that just as human nature is a complex and fallible and sometimes contradictory thing, so too is what's happening in Hardwick. And, quite likely, so too will be any efforts to replicate it.

Because the factors that have given rise to Hardwick's unique place in the story of our nation's shifting agricultural landscape are themselves unique and, in many cases, particularly difficult to quantify. Certainly, we can take measure of the hard assets, the fertile soil and abundant farmland and the businesses that allow the region to draw a circle—crudely, perhaps, but still a circle—of its food system: compost and seed, fruit and vegetable, milk and cheese and the waste from animals and animal processing, which is applied to the land or turned into more compost. To a certain degree, these are components that can be duplicated and scaled for other communities, with adaptations in deference to climate and topography.

As challenging as that might be, it is also the easy part. The harder task—the much, much, much harder task—is to begin to identify the intangibles that have led Hardwick and her people to this place and time. Why has this little, blue-collar town evolved in this way? Is it simple dumb luck that has brought this particular group of people, with their particular skills, together? Is their response to the hardships of their town and of the world beyond its borders merely a commonsense reaction? And if so, why isn't every community responding in a similar manner? Do these people see a future that everyone else is somehow blind to? Is this the workings of the metaphysical force that Tom Stearns refers to?

There are answers to these questions, though they're not always complete. At first glance, they may not even be logical, because answering these questions almost demands that we learn a new language or, at the very least, learn how to use our old language differently. I am sure that I will fumble over some of this; pieces of the whole—some surely critical—will likely elude me. But I will try anyway.

I believe that Hardwick is succeeding not in spite of its relative impoverishment, but *because* of it. What is happening in Hardwick does not happen in the absence of trust and collaboration; it does not happen without a shared sense of destiny. Call it vision, if you want, though I'd rather leave such soaring rhetoric to Tom Stearns. And I believe that this trust and collaboration are in no small ways social and cultural responses to economic hardship. Money does many things very well, and one of those things is to insulate us from each other. It becomes a safety net, and when we carry a safety net made of cash, we allow the one made of community to slip through our fingers. By and large, the people of Hardwick have not had this luxury.

Too, I think Hardwick's size has served it well. It's hard to imagine that a community smaller than 3,200 people could muster the critical mass to get the wheel turning—and keep it turning—on such an ambitious project. I'm equally skeptical that a larger town could have hatched this plan: Moving with such speed and certainty requires a streamlined approach that's readily foiled by too many opinions and the voices attached to those opinions—too many cooks in the kitchen, to use the obvious and appropriate metaphor. This is not to say that the processes being developed and implemented in Hardwick can't be applied to even smaller towns or to communities within cities small and large. It is only to suggest that it is likely that the initial development of these processes requires a particular scale. This is a very human endeavor and Hardwick, clearly, functions on a very human scale.

I wonder if the ability of Hardwick's agriculturists to imagine a future that's quite unlike the present day is at least partly the result of the town's somewhat isolated nature. It is not as if the distractions and trappings of 21st-century American life are absent from Hardwick (heck, as of mid-2009, you could even buy a cell phone in town), but it is true that here, in general, people have more time to reflect and absorb the evolving realities of what the future might look like and how that future might best be greeted. Or maybe, because of the interconnected and interdependent nature of the community, they simply feel safe enough to reflect on and absorb the daunting tasks that face us all. Perhaps it's a little of both, but in any case, it seems to me as if the quiet, connected nature of the town and its people fosters an awareness that is able to both recognize and react to truths that might escape the over-saturated experience of life in contemporary America.

And, more obviously, one cannot ignore the town's deep agricultural underpinnings. It is what people know, and even if many of those driving the current agrepreneurial revolution are not wizened sages of the land, even if they were born to a suburban experience many states away, there can be no denying the sway of Hardwick's agrarian ethic, aesthetic, and knowledge. If the influences that shape a community can be said to fall into the categories of nature and nurture, then it's almost as if Hardwick's community had no other choice: Agriculture infuses both.

What does all this mean for the rest of our country? I began writing this book under the assumption that the specific, tangible components of Hardwick's food system should prove to be replicable: a compost bin for every city, a seed bank for every town. There's something to this. After all, these are vital resources that every community should have, just as they should have a reliable supply of water or a fire department.

But as I've already stated, I've come to believe that it is the process, awareness, and connectedness that will prove to be Hardwick's most valuable lessons. For many decades, humanity has cheated the laws of nature through the hubris of its own intelligence. Or, at least, what we've come to perceive as intelligence, and the technology it has brought forth. We've forgotten that every economy is ultimately an economy that exists only with the blessing of the sun and the land; without these, we have nothing, and no amount of distancing ourselves from this reality will make it true. Yet we have fooled ourselves into believing that we can usurp these forces through the blunt application of wit and will and the technologies they give rise to. For a time, we have been granted the illusion that we can succeed in this task. That time is coming to a close. Change or be changed: These are the choices.

The people of Hardwick have chosen the former. Some chose this long ago; some are coming to it now, in a way that's indicative of their particular time and place. But whatever differences exist, all share at least one thing: the recognition that we have gone so incredibly far astray. Or perhaps we have been led there; it's probably some of each, but either way, it doesn't really matter. The status quo has failed us completely. The symptoms of this failure are everywhere. It's not just our sickly food system and our relationship to it; it's the economic crisis, the dislocation and disenchantment of millions of Americans nationwide, and all the inflated expectations that wrought these failures. In a society that's trying to find its footing on many, many fronts, Hardwick, Vermont, with all its scruff and authenticity, feels like an island of security and sanity, and it occurs to me that of the many important things the rest of America can learn from this little town, how to produce and distribute food might not even be at the top of the list.

Yet there *have* been tangible changes in Hardwick, many provoked by the town's commitment to its food system. There are jobs where once there weren't, there are resources being utilized that once were discarded, there are storefronts being occupied that, not long ago, sat vacant. There is a sense that the town is awakening to its potential and that even if no one knows exactly what that potential looks like, the awakening itself can serve as a catalyst to help the community thrive. These are answers—or at least a certain type of answers—to the question of whether or not Hardwick's agricultural economy is viable. These are answers—or at least the outlines of answers—to the question of whether or not decentralized food systems can be agents of positive change in other communities.

Because it is not merely our small, economically distraught communities that must be saved by food. Indeed, unless we are to place full faith in the magic of exponential growth against a finite resource base, we must recognize that at some point all countries and cultures that have fallen under the spell of industrial agriculture will need to be saved by food. This is a humbling truth. I once believed that local food carried the scent of pretense, but I have come to understand that the posturing is not being done by proponents of local agriculture. Indeed, the real arrogance is the assumption that we can continue getting something for less than it is worth and that our bodies, communities, and lands won't rebel against this falsehood.

Perhaps someday you will drive into the town of Hardwick, Vermont, weaving through that series of curves on the east side of town, rolling down Main Street, past the Buffalo Mountain Food Co-op, past the Center for an Agricultural Economy, past Claire's, and then make that right-hand turn at the town's single blinking light, past the former boxing club, the fire department, the gun shop. Maybe you'll park your car and take a stroll across the walking bridge or push open the door of the co-op to buy a loaf of Charlie Emers's bread and a round of Jasper Hill cheese, a tomato from Pete Johnson, a carrot from Louie Pulver. If so, I suggest you take a seat on one of the benches in the Peace Park where, not so long ago, the town's adult-movie goers gathered. You might sit there and eat, watching the traffic pass, listening to the constant, low murmur of the village and its people. You might consider how it can sometimes seem as if a great deal of what it means to be human has been stripped from our daily lives and how something as simple as the way we eat has the potential to restore so much of what we've lost. Or maybe you just want to enjoy your snack, to feel the sun on your face. That's okay, too.

But even if you never come to Hardwick, I hope that you recognize something of her in your hometown. I hope that you recognize something of her within *yourself,* because the work that awaits us will be done in this quiet way: neighborhood by neighborhood, community by community, person by person, until we are all linked by the very thing that grants us life. Until we have wrested our destiny from a system that is convoluted, hierarchical, and dangerous for the dependence it engenders and planted it in our own communities, in our own soils, with our own hands. Until someday when we can look back and realize it wasn't just a town that food saved: It was a country.

ACKNOWLEDGMENTS

Writing about one's friends and neighbors is a tricky proposition. Fortunately, I am blessed with friends and neighbors who are kind, gracious, and generally tolerant of my incessant badgering and ignorance. These include, in no particular order, Tom Stearns, Tom Gilbert, Ralph and Cindy Persons, Andrew Meyer and the extended Meyer family, Steve Gorelick, Suzanna Jones, the Kehler family, Pete Johnson, Forrest Foster, Karen Shaw, Louie Pulver, Annie Gaillard, Steven Obranovich, and Mike Bosia. Without these people, this book would not have happened; without any one of these people, it would have lacked a crucial degree of color and depth.

Of course, the town of Hardwick and the surrounding communities are more than these few individuals, so I want to express my ongoing gratitude to the people of the region. I've lived in rural northern Vermont for my entire life and it is my intention to die here. The primary reason for my appreciation of the area is the people who make me proud to live among them.

I want to thank my agents, Joanna Stampfel-Volpe and Peter Rubie, who took a shot on an unproven writer from the sticks. It was wicked decent of them. Ditto my editors at Rodale, Colin Dickerman and Gena Smith. It would be foolish to suggest that selling and writing a book can be easy; it would be equally foolish not to acknowledge that without the wise guidance of these good people it would have been a heck of a lot harder. And exponentially less readable.

Finally, for reading many drafts and putting up with my constant babble on all matters Hardwick and food, thank you Penny. Playing in the dirt wouldn't be nearly as much fun without you.

Shelton State Libraries
Shelton State Community College